Anytime, Anywhere

Anytime, Anywhere
Sharing Faith Jesus Style

William L. Turner

Judson Press ® Valley Forge

Anytime, Anywhere: Sharing Faith Jesus Style
© 1997 Judson Press, Valley Forge, PA 19482-0851

Bible quotations in this volume are from the New Revised Standard Version, copyright © 1989 by the Division of Christian Education of the National Council of the Churches of Christ in the United States of America. Used by permission. All rights reserved.

Library of Congress Cataloging-in-Publication Data
Turner, William L., 1938-
    Anytime, anywhere : sharing faith Jesus style / William L. Turner.
      p. cm.
    Includes bibliographical references.
    ISBN 0-8170-1260-5 (alk. paper)
    1. Witness bearing (Christianity) 2. Jesus Christ—Evangelistic methods. 3. Witness bearing (Christianity) in the Bible.
    I. Title
BV4520.T75 1997
248'.5—dc21   96-39600

Printed in the U.S.A.

05 04 03 02 01 00 99 98 97

10 9 8 7 6 5 4 3 2 1

*To the family of South Main Baptist Church
with love and gratitude*

Contents

Acknowledgments

Because no book is ever the work of a single individual, there are people to be thanked. Some of my earliest teachers instilled in me an interest in holistic personal evangelism. "Soul winning" for them was never about the rescue of some disembodied spirit. It was about enlisting the total person in personal faith and a growing, ministering discipleship. Sabin Landry, Wayne Oates, Findley Edge, Henlee Barnette, Dale Moody, William Hull, and Samuel Southard were important contributors to my concept of faith sharing. My loving wife, Kelli, has offered great feedback on this project. She was the first person to begin reading the manuscript and has consistently offered both keen insight and warm encouragement. I'm grateful to my colleagues on the ministerial staff at South Main for their initial encouragement to publish this volume. Linda Gardner is an excellent pastor's secretary whose typing and editing skills are reflected in these pages. Not reflected, but of equal importance, is her great patience with the publication process—and with me. I am also grateful to Judson Press and to Kristy Pullen, Victoria McGoey, and Mary Nicol, who believed that this book on evangelism might find a niche in today's marketplace. They have been helpful partners.

Finally, I want to express my deep gratitude to the people who have nurtured and challenged me for nearly a dozen years: the members of South Main Baptist Church. Their encouragement of my ministry in all its expressions has been strong and consistent. I am blessed indeed to labor among them.

Introduction

There are three assumptions behind what I want to say in this book. The first assumption is that the kingdom of God grows in large part because of the witness of its members. As an everyday, hands-on microcosm of the kingdom, a local congregation either grows or does not grow in direct proportion to whether its members do or do not share their faith with unchurched people. The second assumption is that American Christians now find themselves in a true first-century situation, since the cultural accumulation of Christian values and Christian knowledge has withered in our society. My third assumption is that our Lord Jesus Christ can help us learn to share our faith and extend God's kingdom. We have the guidance of his Spirit within us and among us, of course, but the New Testament contains actual stories of Jesus' life. In the following pages we will address two central questions: (1) how did Jesus share his faith and (2) what can you and I learn about doing that *now* from *him?*

There is a lot of biblical support for the first assumption—that our personal witness is crucial to God's kingdom. Jesus sends out his first disciples on a mission tour (Luke 10:1-20). At the end of his ministry he gives the Great Commission (Matthew 28:19-20). "As you're going into the world," he says, "make disciples." Luke's version of Jesus' commission to the disciples in Acts 1 recalls that Jesus says, "You shall be my witnesses, beginning in Jerusalem . . . and to the uttermost parts of the earth" (Acts 1:8). Evidently more than a few people believed him! The rest of the New Testament testifies to that.

Edward Gibbon, writing about the decline and fall of the Roman Empire, concluded that early Christianity spread so rapidly because the people who became believers felt that it was their sacred duty to share the blessings they had received with their friends and relatives. I doubt that 100 percent of them participated in witnessing, but obviously many of those new believers led nonbelievers to faith in Christ.

One of our problems now is that most of us are not new believers. A lot of us came to faith years ago, and we have worked at the life of discipleship ever since. A lifetime of learning is involved in living the Christian faith. In one of his "On the Road" books, Charles Kuralt remembers a conversation with American painter Andrew Wyeth. After they had looked out over the Pennsylvania landscape in silence for a few moments, Wyeth spoke about his love of the land. He talked about the valley, the hill, and the land on top of the hill. Then he said, "I just find the more I look, the more I see, the more I feel, and I want to go deeper." Then in a most telling sentence, Wyeth said, "I have not exhausted the ground I stand on . . ."[1] That is true of every Christian I know! When it comes to the depths of faith, there is always more to be known. No matter how much ground we cover, the amount left to cover is truly inexhaustible.

But Christian faith is not just a deeply inward journey. It's not about better, clearer understanding only. It's also about passing on to others what we know and about inviting them to join the journey of faith. And if we don't do that, our own inner growth will be stunted and our faith will remain underdeveloped.

The Library of Congress contains several priceless Stradivarius violins—objects of art and beauty. Every week musicians come in and play them. If these violins were not played, they would soon deteriorate. Even as a Stradivarius has to be played, the Christian faith has to be shared, or it too will deteriorate. We spend a lot of time polishing, refining, and taking care of this instrument—our faith—but it needs to be played as well.

Clearly we are called to be witnesses to our faith. But most of us are not very intentional about it. There are some reasons for our inactivity. We don't know non-Christians because we spend most of our time with fellow believers. We're not sure we know how to do it. We don't feel comfortable. Witnessing could be embarrassing, awkward, or offensive to the other person. It feels unnatural, somehow. So we let it go. Somebody else will do it . . . maybe.

My longtime Alabama friend, Hudson Baggett, liked to tell the story about a revival meeting during which a church member, a barber, made a commitment to speak to someone about becoming a Christian within the next week. He waited and waited, fretting about how to do it, until the very end of the week. Late on Saturday afternoon, as his last customer came in, he realized this would be his only opportunity. Nervously, he prepared the man in the chair and stretched him out for a shave. As he stropped the razor, he tried to think of what to say. Finally, looking down at the man and holding the razor in full view, he asked in a strained voice, "Are you ready to die?" The man jumped up and ran for his life! Personal witnessing can be embarrassing!

A few years ago I heard Dale Bruner, who teaches at a Christian college in Spokane, Washington, tell about his own attempts at personal evangelism. Inspired by a respected Bible teacher, he set out to share his faith. First he sat on a park bench with a man who was obviously a Marine. Turning to the Marine he asked, "Have you ever thought about Jesus Christ?" The Marine looked at him and said, "If you don't get out of here in two minutes, I'm going to smash your face in!" Dale got out of there and went to a bus stop where he found an older man. Thinking that a friendly and less direct conversation might be more effective, he started to talk with him. They spoke about the day, the weather, and other things. Before he could get more deeply into the conversation, however, a bus came and took the man away! These horror stories, and many others like them, tend to reinforce our reluctance to share our faith. But the mandate remains.

The second assumption stated at the beginning of this chapter is that we are carrying out church outreach and personal evangelism in a context that is similar to the first-century situation.

America is now the fifth-largest unchurched nation in the world. In Texas, where I live, there are more unchurched people than there are in fifty-two other *countries* and in forty-two other states. One recent survey of Harris County (in which Houston is located) revealed that 70 percent of our population is unchurched ("churched" was defined as attending a church event twice a month). Our culture is largely secular, pluralistic, and unchurched. That's a first-century situation!

We don't have the Holy Roman Empire of the Middle Ages. We don't have the culture of Christendom that followed it. We don't have the Puritan culture of early America. We don't even have the Protestant consensus of the nineteenth century. "The Bible Belt is gone," a pastor friend in an old South metropolis told me recently. We are doing church in a different age, and the gospel, when it is heard, understood, and accepted, will be something fresh and radical in this culture.

Who are these pluralistic, secular, unchurched persons? George Hunter, a teacher at Kentucky's Asbury Seminary, targets several characteristics of today's unchurched Americans.[2] Here are four of them.

1. These persons are essentially *ignorant of basic Christianity.* Better than 90 percent of Americans believe in God, and that statistic hasn't changed much in the last fifty years. Many say they attended church as children and sometimes pray. But Christianity as a personal confession of need and acceptance of grace, they know not. A lot of these folks were exposed early in their lives to either a harsh or a diluted version of Christian faith, and that has served to inoculate them against the real thing . . . so far. Basic Christianity is something fresh and new.

2. They are *looking for life before death.* They're not completely unconcerned about what happens to us when we die. I've noticed, for example, that they tend to be careful listeners at memorial services. For a few minutes they will think with me or some other pastor about life and death and hope. But, by and large, they are hungry for meaning and direction right now.

3. They *see things as being out of control.* There's a deep sense of "I can't fix it anymore and I'm looking for somebody who can." Sam Shoemaker used to say that almost everybody has a problem, is a problem, or lives with a problem. Their slick appearances to the contrary, these people are ready to agree with Shoemaker, acknowledging that things are not right either in society or in their own lives.

4. They *don't know how to get help.* They are on their own, and they are searching. They respond to almost anything on the faith spectrum—from strange fundamentalisms to New Age and beyond—that offers help. Interestingly enough, in this secular age, the spiritual smorgasbord is sumptuous. Boston College philosopher and Catholic layman Peter Kreeft sees genuine spiritual hunger on his university campus, where his classes on angels fill up quickly. He warns, however, that society's sudden interest in angels may be junk food for the soul ("McAngels," he terms them).[3] Though quite orthodox in his personal views, Kreeft worries that today's angel fad offers "the thrill of religion without the inconvenience of it."[4] New Agers of various sorts now make up about 7 percent of our national population. When that movement fades, something similar will surely replace it. A lot of people join twelve-step groups. There are more than two hundred different kinds now, some related to churches and some not. Others join health clubs or spas or meditation circles or reading groups or self-help seminars. G. K. Chesterton's famous dictum says it well: When people stop believing in God, they don't believe in nothing; they believe in anything. Unchurched Americans aren't sure how to get help, but they are looking . . . furiously.

Norman Lear, the television producer who gave us *All in the Family, Sanford and Son,* and *One Day at a Time,* among other programs, is Jewish and classifies himself as "an unaffiliated groper" in matters of religion. In December 1993, speaking to a Washington, D.C., audience, Lear talked about the disconnected, buzzing eruption of spiritual reaction to our times. Despite the arrogance of secularism, as well as of some established religion, Lear sees millions of gropers among us who are just plain hungry for spiritual reality.

I was moved by a Douglas Coupland essay that refers to "losing God" and "a world without religion" with obvious sadness. His melancholy words deserve to be read slowly and carefully:

> *I think I am a broken person. I seriously question the road my life has taken, and I endlessly rehash the compromises I have made in my life. I have an unsecure and vaguely crappy job with an amoral corporation so that I don't have to worry about money. I put up with half-way relationships so as not to have to worry about loneliness. I have lost the ability to recapture the purer feelings of my younger years in exchange for a streamlined narrow-mindedness that I assumed would propel me to "the top." What a joke.[5]*

Coupland confesses a deep yearning. "Sometimes I just feel that there must be another road that I can walk down—away from this person I became, either against my will or by default."[6] Finally, in a rare moment of openness, he reveals his hidden hunger:

> *My secret is that I need God—that I am sick and can no longer make it alone. I need God to help me give, because I no longer seem to be capable of giving; to help me be kind, as I no longer seem capable of kindness; to help me love, as I seem beyond being able to love.[7]*

To George Hunter's list, let me add other characteristics that I have observed about unchurched Americans. First of all, they live in cities. Seventy-five percent of the American people live in our metropolitan areas, and 72 percent of this crowd is unchurched. We must not exclude rural areas and small towns, especially with "out-migration" boosting their populations. Still, most unchurched people remain concentrated in our large cities.

Unchurched Americans, young and old, are mobile. The baby boomers (aged fifty and under) number 76 million. The next generation (the baby busters) are more than 60 million. These two groups together make up the largest segment of our population, and they're on the go. One in five Americans moves to a new location every year. Though two-income families and a sometimes stagnant economy have slowed the rate of mobility somewhat, the average American family can still expect to relocate between ten and fifteen times in a lifetime. Of course, there are plenty of unchurched people in the older generation too. They also are more mobile than ever, thanks to better health, longer life after retirement, and a dramatic increase in travel opportunities.

Unchurched Americans are also single. Single adults now make up 52 percent of our national population. Many are students, and the median college age keeps going up. Others are widows and widowers. Many are single working parents. Most are straight, but some are homosexual. Many are immigrants (we speak 350 different languages every day in America). Many are poor, including a disproportionate number of children.

Unchurched Americans are also married couples and unmarried couples living together with and without the benefit of license and clergy.

Unchurched Americans are interested in spiritual issues. They believe in God (or fate or something) because it makes sense—or because they're afraid not to. They are sometimes superstitious, and they are often followers of spiritual fads. But the hunger for spirituality among unchurched Americans is evident from the movies they see to the support groups they attend to the books they read. One weekend early in 1995, I conducted my own informal study of the New York *Times* best-seller list. I counted ten books that deal with spirituality. Pope John Paul II's book, *Crossing the Threshhold of Hope,* led the nonfiction list, and *The Celestine Prophecy*, by James Redfield, was the leader in fiction. By early 1995, Scott Peck's book *The Road Less Traveled* had been on the best-seller list for 585 consecutive weeks. Unchurched Americans do care about spiritual matters. They're concerned about their children's spiritual training. And now many of them (before they hit the midlife crisis) are asking, "Is this how I want to live the rest of my life . . . in the pursuit of sex and sports and the accumulation of stuff and weekends?"

Also characteristic of unchurched Americans is that they attend church sporadically and occasionally. Institutional religion bumps into their lives from time to time—for a wedding, a funeral, or a holiday worship service. A sense of social obligation still seats a few of these folks in our pews, while job expectation corrals a few others from time to time. Film critic Michael Medved sometimes plays a game at Hollywood parties. He likes to ask people how many Americans they think go to church every week. "No one I know," is usually the first response he gets. When he persists, these Hollywood types usually guess about 1 percent. The highest guess he has ever heard is 10 percent. Actually, 43 percent of Americans attend church on any given weekend—more than watch the Super Bowl.[8]

Unchurched Americans don't necessarily see themselves as "non-Christians." Seventy-seven percent of them have just quit church. They're not belongers anymore, but they're still believers—sort of. Many think of America as a "Christian nation" with a civil religion. Others have some memory of what they used to believe, but the institution of the church has somehow lost meaning and credibility for them.

Finally, the unchurched American is not very literate about the Bible. A 1994 survey of twelve hundred people, ages 15 to 35, revealed that most of those asked could name no more than two of the Ten Commandments. In addition, *Atlantic Monthly* writer Cullen Murphy says, "The weren't too happy about some of the others when they were told about them."[9]

I once heard author and television commentator Bill Moyers describe an experience he had in Manhattan in 1968. Having left the Johnson White House, he moved to New York City to become editor of *Newsday*. Wanting to get a feel for his new surroundings, Moyers got in his car for a drive around the city and its outlying areas. He picked a day when a fierce Atlantic storm was blowing in, so after a while he parked his car and dashed into a wayside diner. The only other person inside was a waitress, and Moyers tried to strike up a conversation with her. "Some weather," he exclaimed. "Yep," she said. After a moment or two he ventured, "I don't know when I've seen wind this strong." "Uh-huh," was her response. Finally he said, "I doubt there's been any rain this heavy since the Flood." "Excuse me," the waitress said, "What flood?" "You know," said Moyers, "the big Flood with forty days and forty nights of rain." The waitress quickly responded, "Look, Mister, I haven't watched television in over a week!"

Yokefellow Movement leader James Newby recalls an additional illustration. He was being interviewed by a newspaper reporter about the history of the Yokefellow Movement. To provide some background, Newby quoted the great "yoke" passage from Matthew 11:28-30: "Come to me all who labor and are heavy-laden, and I will give you rest. Take my yoke upon you and learn from me: for I am gentle and lowly in heart, and you will find rest for your souls. For my yoke is easy and my burden is light." The reporter responded, "That's beautiful. Are you quoting from someone, or did you write that yourself?" Newby looked for a twinkle in the man's eye that would reveal a hint of sarcasm. But the man continued to stare at him straight-faced, waiting for a response. Interestingly, this particular man was the "religion reporter" for his newspaper![10]

The Gallup organization finds that only half of all Americans can name the Bible's first book. Only 21 percent can name a single Old Testament prophet. Only a third of all adults know that it was Jesus who delivered the Sermon on the Mount. In the face of all of this, one of the paradigm shifts that is happening in our culture is that "come-to" strategies are less and less effective in church growth and personal evangelism. As in the first century, it's a "go-to" situation. If, as current statistics strongly suggest, half of all American adults will have no church background by the year 2000, the friendships between Christians and non-Christians will be of enormous importance.

That brings us to my third assumption, namely, that Jesus can help us learn to share our faith and extend God's kingdom. Of course, he preached sermons, told parables, and did extended teaching—often addressing sizable crowds. But he also had one-on-one encounters with individuals. Unlike other holy men and gurus, Jesus doesn't camp on a mountaintop or in a secluded temple waiting for people to seek him out regarding the spiritual issues of life. He travels through the countryside and roams the city streets, rubbing elbows with people and meeting spiritual needs where they surface in their day-to-day lives. Though he doesn't expect a majority to flock to his message (Matthew 7:13-14), Jesus consistently shares his faith and convictions about God and human beings with the people he meets.

The relevance of Jesus as a model is obvious. Statistics clearly show that more people are led to Christian faith and active involvement in the life of a church through interpersonal contacts than through all other methods of outreach combined. Given the busy schedule of today's active churches, plus our tendency to spend most of our time with other Christians, the reality is that most of us have very little contact with unbelievers! I hope that these pages will make you more intentional about cultivating relationships with unchurched persons. Unless we do, the chances of ever having the opportunity to share the gospel and church fellowship are so slim as to be virtually nonexistent. If, on the other hand, we get to know people in the context of friendship and neighborliness, we have at least opened the door to a wonderful possibility.

It is in Jesus' prayer life that we find a real key to preparation for and sensitivity to his daily encounters. Jesus took each context seriously . . . and each one was different. He did not share his faith verbally with everybody he met, nor with everybody in the same way. A few set formulas and methods cannot address every situation. With Jesus it was sometimes a dinner conversation, sometimes a roadside encounter, sometimes a one-time meeting, other times a long-term relationship. Prayer and attention to context are two important lessons we can learn from Jesus.

The conclusion is inescapable: Jesus was a faith sharer. It's time now to look at the evidence more closely. It's time to learn . . . and to follow!

Notes

1. Charles Kuralt, *A Life on the Road* (New York: G. P. Putnam's Sons, 1990), pp. 211-12.

2. George G. Hunter III, *How to Reach Secular People* (Nashville: Abingdon, 1992), pp. 44-54.

3. "Angel-Mania Offers a 'Thrill of Religion,'" *Austin American-Statesman,* 25 April 1996, p. E2.

4. Ibid.

5. Douglas Coupland, "Starting Over with God," *The Utne Reader* 75 (June 1996): 34.

6. Ibid.

7. Ibid.

8. Cited in Michael Novak, "Steeple Envy," *Forbes,* 5 July 1993, p. 46.

9. John Leo, "Thou shalt not command," *U.S. News and World Report*, 18 November, 1996, p. 16.

10. *Quarterly Yoke Letter* 38, no. 4 (December 1995): 1.

CHAPTER 1

With His Family

Mark 3:31-35

The second chapter of Luke contains the story of Jesus' birth, the family's return to Nazareth, and their trip to the temple when Jesus was twelve. After that, his family all but disappears from the New Testament record. His mother pops in and out of the story more than anybody else. She is present at the wedding at Cana, and she shows up at the cross (probably heartbroken and confused, but there). His father we don't hear about at all after Jesus' birth and childhood; speculation is strong that he may have died long before Jesus was grown. His brothers, four of them, are named in the Gospels, and his sisters, unfortunately and unfairly, are not.

Three Gospel writers, however, remember a time when Jesus' family showed up (Mark 3:31-35; Matthew 12:45-50; Luke 8:19-21). In Mark's account it happens early in Jesus' ministry. The disciples have been called, the crowds are growing, but he is already controversial. The people who should have understood him first and best (his family and the teachers of the law) didn't.

It's easy to see why. He is baptized by that radical John in the Jordan River; he touches lepers and paralytics who are unclean (sinners); he blasphemously talks about forgiving people's sins; he gathers around him not the scholars and the holy men, but a motley crew of Galilean fishermen, a Roman tax collector, and some women of questionable reputation. And the sabbath? He "works" by healing people. He also "harvests" on the sabbath by plucking grain in the fields as he's passing through.

All of this Mark records in his first two and a half chapters, and Jesus is just getting warmed up! So people are saying, "He's gone back on his good Jewish raisin'," or, "He's lost it!" That's when his family shows up, probably to take him home, calm him down, and check him out. They just didn't get it, not for a long time. In John's Gospel, when he's a little deeper into his ministry, his brothers have seen some miraculous works but they're still unsure, still testing him. So they urge him to leave the obscurity of Galilee and go back to the limelight and high exposure of Jerusalem. He tells them no, that he's on a different timetable. And the text says, "Not even his brothers believed in him" (John 7:5).

So what's to be learned about faith and family from Jesus? Two things at least. First, *he shared their faith.* His family is where he learned to believe. It may be where you learned to believe as well. No consideration of personal evangelism ought to leave out the family. Boys and girls and moms and dads by the thousands are led to faith by the teaching and the interaction at home. A show of hands in any Sunday morning worship crowd would reveal that most of us who are Christians came to that choice before we were eighteen years old. Some of the rest of us would raise our hands and talk about being baptized with our children. Others would speak about the influence of a spouse in leading us to Christ. A home where people of faith live is a "field white unto harvest" for Christian witness. By the time he's twelve, Jesus is in Jerusalem talking about doing his "Father's business." Where did he get that? In Nazareth, at home.

What did Jesus learn at home? Listen to his stories and you'll know that he spent time with both parents—in the kitchen and in the carpenter's shop. He's knowledgeable about yokes that fit, about leaven, and about seasoning. He understands about not putting wine into old wineskins. He's grown up with the lilies of the field and people sowing seed. He's watched birds nesting and sheep grazing and vineyard workers pruning. He's seen prodigal sons and daughters, and he's probably piped, danced, and played with his brothers and sisters in village streets.

Listen to his stories and you will know that he learned early about a faith that is for real, live human beings—ordinary folks like poor widows, money lenders, tax collectors, even Samaritans. Listen to his stories and you will know that he has been nurtured in a relationship with God that is not for lofty moments alone but is grounded in day-to-day interaction with parents and siblings, in the study of Hebrew Scriptures, in dialogue with a small-town rabbi whose identity we'll never know.

In that Nazareth family, he learns how to handle forgiveness and reconciliation. Mary keeps a lot in her heart and to herself. Do people in Nazareth know about his mysterious birth? Has anybody used the word *illegitimate*? Does Jesus grow up feeling like an outsider? He learns Scripture, prayer, and curiosity at home. He also learns about love and faith, tenderness and anger, grace and forgiveness.

See how he treats women in a brutally chauvinistic world, and you'll know the strong dignity of his mother. Listen as he makes *father* his most natural word for God, and you'll know something of the man Joseph was, how he and his children shared life. Someone has suggested that Jesus became a great person because Joseph, his father, treated him as if he were a child of God. What a great father-son model *that* is! When Jesus came to focus on his heavenly Father's business at age twelve, it was because he had shared and learned faith in a family.

As Loren Mead points out, Jesus' life takes a radical new turn at the time of his encounter with John the Baptist. By that time, says Mead:

> *His mind held the words of the Psalms—memorized from weekly and daily recitation. He had heard stories of the Maccabees from the older people of his village. His mother had taught him strange stories of her own encounters with God. He knew the words of Isaiah and had struggled with their meanings. He had*

heard other stories from his rabbis. So when his moment of transformation and call occurred, he had at his disposal the words and images to define his vocation and shape his work. He had the raw material ready at hand.[1]

Don't ever underestimate this first context for witness. We are privileged to be the first evangelists our children and families ever have. When it comes to sharing our faith with our children, the best method seems to be more relational than informational. It's obvious that Jesus received Scripture and other teaching in his Nazareth home, but the most telling part of his formative years may well have been his personal relationship with parents of spiritual integrity. Eighty years ago, writing his classic *Christian Nurture,* Horace Bushnell described parental character as an ever flowing stream that washes over the life of a child. Our verbal admonitions and moral lectures, he says, are but ripples on that stream. His conclusion? "If you expect your child to go with the ripple instead of the stream, you will be disappointed."[2] Children really do learn what they live with, and one of our greatest opportunities is to share our spiritual values with them in the way we treat them. Our social, cultural, and spiritual values are the first that our children have any contact with.

In the summer of 1992 my wife, Kelli, and I were at Laity Lodge in the Texas hill country with about thirty other people for a week of contemplation, prayer, and study. Our opening session fell on the evening of Father's Day, and during the time of introduction we were each asked to remember our own fathers and say a few words about them. I spoke about how my dad had given me a sense of humor and had slept through most of the sermons he'd ever heard, teaching me early on not to take myself too seriously. Members of the group spoke words of warmth and praise for fathers, as well as words of hostility and grief. I was especially moved by the words of one young woman who said, "My father died fourteen years ago, and I feel like I know him better now than I ever did while he was alive." Her statement jarred me as I thought about my own mortality and the legacy I am leaving to my children and grandchildren. Her words provoked thoughts like, Have I let them know me? Do they understand my values and why I hold them? Have I been open and vulnerable with them? The next day I spotted the young woman on campus. As I fell into step beside her, I said, "Your statement last night really scared me. Would you mind telling me what you meant by it?" And through some tears (she was still grieving her mother's recent death), she recalled that her father had been alcoholic, busy, and distant. She described a man who never seemed to have time for her emotionally. She said, "I guess he didn't think enough of himself to believe that anything he might want to say to me would have any value."

To use Myron Madden's classification, this young woman was an *unblessed child.* She was unblessed by a parent who couldn't let her inside his defenses, couldn't be vulnerable, couldn't share himself with his daughter. Looking back as an adult, she understands him better, though some of the pain of that missed opportunity remains.

More than thirty years ago now, someone handed me a copy of a child's prayer. In a few well-chosen words, it describes the family soil in which meaningful faith can grow:

> *O God, you are so great and I am so small, and there's so much about you that I do not understand. But then perhaps I understand, at least a little. When I am glad because I know my father and mother love me, is it you who made them love? When I try harder because they trust me, is it you who made them trust? If so, then I know that I can love you, and I want to love you more and more. Amen.*

Albert Schweitzer's observation is worth remembering. "There are only three ways to teach a child: the first is by example, the second is by example, the third is by example."[3]

There is at least one other thing to be learned about Jesus' faith and his family, namely, *he chose a growing faith.* It's certainly true that Jesus, like every child in a religious household, grew to that time in his life when he chose "his father's business"—his personal faith. As a pastor, I relish those moments when I sit with young people to discuss their baptism. Often I hear statements like "I was sitting in church last week and decided it was time for me to accept Christ." "At camp this week, I realized that I needed to make a decision." "I've been thinking about this for quite a while. It's time I trusted Christ."

But salvation is more than a decision; it's a journey toward growth and understanding. I like the way Tex Sample puts it. "That God accepts us as we are is the good news; that God is not through with us at this point is the call to discipleship."[4] Such a pattern is clear in the life of Jesus. His bar mitzvah is past, his adulthood has begun, and he begins to grow into a faith that is uniquely personal. Basically, that's what the description of the visit by Jesus' family is about—his enlarged faith, not the rejection of his family of origin. It is about expanding that family to include all of those who will live by faith. "Whoever does the will of God is my brother and sister and mother," he says. We are included! We are Christ's family, learning to live out God's will and purpose for us. Jesus is the first to refer to a faith community as "brothers" and "sisters." "You're my family"—blessed words! Jesus made his faith choice, and it went beyond his family of origin, even beyond his Jewishness. No wonder his family thought he was listing toward unreality. He envisions a family that is radically different!

I am sure one reason Matthew, Mark, and Luke all record this particular family encounter is that by the time the Gospels were being written down, a lot of believers were being ridiculed and rejected by their families and friends because they had come to faith in Christ. The message in this little story is crystal clear. "You're not alone. You belong to the family of Christ. Jew, Gentile, male, female, slave, free—you *belong* among your brothers and sisters in Christ!" A lot of people in early Christianity needed that kind of reassurance.

People still do.

I was at a young man's bedside one afternoon because he was

dying of AIDS. Our church's ministry group to AIDS patients and their families had been taking care of him. He had attended worship in our church a few times and had privately acknowledged his need for God's forgiveness. On that weekday afternoon he confided to me that some days before he had committed his life to Christ while sitting in a worship service in our church. He had not been physically able to get down the aisle at the close of that service, but he now told me of his peace and assurance in God's salvation. We prayed together, we hugged, and we spoke of the possibility of his baptism (he never gained enough strength for that). The most painful part of our conversation, for me, was what he said about his parents. They lived in a different state and had not visited him, even when his illness entered its final phase. He had not been welcome "back home" for a long time, and thus his parents' rejection of him, their homosexual son, was complete. He spoke with sadness about that, but he also spoke with deep gratitude for the individuals in our ministry. "They've been great," he said, "loving me and staying with me." He went on to share the details of our members' hands-on ministry.

When he died a few weeks later, I helped conduct his funeral. Our church members and a few other friends were present. Conspicuously absent were parents and family. I hoped that they would be there—back home—to receive his frail remains for burial.

In his hour of need my young friend found that the family of Christ extended him caring and support. That didn't eliminate the pain of being rejected by his family of origin . . . but it did welcome him into another family!

In almost any church family, large or small, you'll meet dozens of people, young and old, who find support and encouragement among Christian believers that they haven't found any place else, including their homes. Last year I met a young man who had grown up in a terribly dysfunctional family with a violent father and an alcoholic mother. When he was five, a neighborhood friend invited him to Sunday school. What he remembers most is the flannelboard and the first lesson he heard about a man named Jesus who loved children. It was the first time in his young life he had heard the word *love*. After that first visit, he never missed a Sunday at the little church a block away. He would ride his bike there during the week to peer through the windows, looking for the man who loved children. On nights when home was unsafe, he would run away from his angry father, crawl through an unlatched Sunday school room window, and sit in front of the flannelboard. Occasionally he would fall asleep there, waking up the next morning to run home and dress for school.

Over time, my young friend became a Christian, entered counseling, and began to use his considerable talents in ministry. He played an instrumental role in the conversion of both parents and in building bridges of forgiveness and reconciliation toward them. "There is nothing too painful or too hard to go through," he now tells college students. "My life gets better, and more free day by day, as I discover who I am in Jesus Christ."

And it all began when a young boy walked into a Sunday school classroom, where some people offered a love that he had never known in his family of origin.

Jesus learned about God and life and faith first in his family, but he chose a faith that stretched his understanding to include a new family. It's a family we now know well, one in which the water of baptism is thicker than the blood of our biological or adoptive connections. That certainly doesn't eliminate immediate family as a high priority for Christians, but it does mean that human love and loyalty work best when they're subject to a higher love and loyalty.

The book of Acts tells us that Jesus' brothers became believers after his resurrection. So Jesus chose personal faith, shared it, and in time, they believed. One of the more interesting facts in New Testament history is that one of those who favored opening church fellowship to everyone—Gentiles as well as Jews—was

James, the Lord's brother (Acts 15:13-21). So he grew later to the enlarged faith that Jesus had chosen earlier.

Today's hymnals have made the words of John Oxenham's hymn, "In Christ There Is No East or West," more inclusive. They are still wonderfully true:

> *Join hands, then, children of the faith,*
> *Whate'er your race may be;*
> *Who serves my father as a child,*
> *Is surely kin to me.*

That's the faith that grew out of family and into family for Jesus. It's the faith he chose . . . and shared.

Notes

1. Loren B. Mead, *Transforming Congregations for the Future* (New York: Alban Institute, 1994), p. 61.

2. Horace Bushnell, *Christian Nuture* (New York: Charles Scribner's Sons, 1916), p. 98.

3. Cited in Richard J. Foster, *Money, Sex, and Power* (San Francisco: Harper and Row, 1985), p. 84.

4. Tex Sample, *U.S. Lifestyles and Mainline Churches* (Louisville: Westminster/John Knox, 1990), p. 133.

CHAPTER 2

At a Rest Stop

John 4:1-42

That Christian faith is to be shared with others is a New Testament given. The earliest learners become apostles, and they are sent out to tell others the story more than once. The church emerges and is given a grand commission to make disciples not just of one group, but of all nations. Jesus himself provides the best model of faith sharing.

The story in John 4 takes place while Jesus is in transition. He leaves Judea and starts back to Galilee. He goes through a Samaritan city called Sychar, the site of Jacob's ancient well. While he's resting at that well, a Samaritan woman comes to draw water. He asks her for a drink.

A rest stop at a water well when you're just passing through is not the most likely place for a spiritually significant event. It's like having a moment of spiritual significance at the laundromat, at the service station, in the parking lot, or at the grocery store. This story out of Jesus' life tells us not to rule out "unlikely" places as settings for spiritual encounters!

Like today's pluralistic America, the setting for this story is a diverse culture. The Samaritans and the Jews had been estranged for eight hundred years, prejudice so ancient that few remembered why it ever started. There had been no temple at Gerizim for a hundred years, but this Samaritan woman remembered that there had once been a place of worship there. Samaria was also a religious culture, which included plenty of individual belief and a lot of superstition and ignorance. As Jesus and this woman talk, she recalls some of the differences and the similarities. This setting is not so very different from our own.

Notice how Jesus shares his faith in that setting. Incidentally, I am convinced that we are told only part of this story by John's Gospel. The woman says, "He told me everything I've ever done." That implies a much longer conversation than John records. Jesus stayed in this village two additional days, but we're given no information about what happened during that time.

But here's what I see: *Jesus is intentional.* Verse 4 says that "he had to go through Samaria." Truth to tell, he didn't. He could have done what most really orthodox people would have done— he could have gone around and crossed over into Galilee north of Samaria. But that would take twice as long, so Jesus chose to go through Samaria—maybe not to save time, but to save people, as he had opportunity. The point is that Jesus put himself in a context where he might encounter a person hungry for God.

Where is that for you and me? Most likely, it's with the people we know away from church. My children's school, my neighborhood, my job, the clubs to which I belong, the committees and boards on which I serve. There are also the regular stops where I shop, where I see service station attendants and store clerks and checkout counter people. If I'm following Jesus' model, *these* are the people I'm going to put myself in a place to get to know. He chose to go through Samaria, and when he got there, he broke out of the "holy huddle" of the disciple band. Verse 8 says that the disciples left to buy food. I suspect that he sent them away. At any rate, he's there at the rest stop, separated from his "holy huddle" on purpose.

The "holy huddle" is a great and necessary thing for our support and nurture in Christian living because it's tough and brutal out there in today's marketplace. Still, Jesus' example here is to be intentional about breaking out of that and getting into the places and with the people who are not part of it. The work colleague who is recently bereaved or divorced or has just been handed a pink slip, for instance. The classmate who is obviously lonely and detached. The individual who just moved into an office down the hall or the family that just moved into a house down the street. There's also the high-energy person who is restless to find a cause and a focus for her life. These are the people I want to drink coffee with, go to lunch with, swap some stories with, listen to, and share my faith with.

Today's nonbelievers, lost and unable to find a focus for their lives, do not respond to "typical" methods of outreach. They probably won't attend revival meetings, probably won't welcome door-to-door visits, and probably don't watch much religious television. They won't respond very positively to religious billboards or bumper stickers. They can be reached, however, by us and by intention and by time. Using those three resources, we may establish and cultivate relationships with people with the goal of winning the right to be heard eventually. One problem most of us have is that we actually know and have contact with so few unbelievers. Socially and personally, we have contact with an awful lot of other Christians. There's nothing wrong with that, of course, but if we're going to reach unchurched Americans, we must, like Jesus, be intentional about building relationships with them.

We're also mighty busy going to church and doing church activities. There's nothing wrong with that, either, but we need to evaluate how we spend our time with a view to reclaiming some of it—even when it's taken up by good causes. It takes time and intention to cultivate relationships and to nurture people toward faith in Christ. "Passing through Samaria" was a choice for Jesus. It must be for us as well.

There's something else here: *Jesus starts with his own humanity.* "Could you give me a drink of water?" That's the first thing Jesus says to this woman. "I'm hungry and tired and thirsty.

Everybody gets that way now and then. Can we establish common ground here?" The Son of God, the Savior of the world does *not* need to be superhuman and above personal vulnerability in order to start sharing his faith. He actually wants to get on the same page with this woman. She's a bit suspicious. "Jews have no dealings with Samaritans." This one did! Circumspect and orthodox men didn't converse with women —even their own wives—in a public place. This one did! A Samaritan's water jar and utensils would be ritually unclean. It didn't matter. "Could I have a drink?" he asked.

You don't have to lead from strength or have all the answers to share your faith. Just be human—just be real. There's a lot of common ground that you share with every person everywhere. Find it! Jesus did.

He also *found a way to communicate that was not prepackaged.* Jesus was great about taking his cues for language from the moment and the person before him. I suspect that one of the reasons he did this so well was that he spent a lot of time in prayer. So attuned was he to the leadership of God's Spirit for his hours and days that he was able to seize faith-sharing opportunities that most people would not have recognized as opportunities. If you and I are serious about sharing the faith, then we must also be serious about prayer and reflection.

The problem with most memorized "plans of salvation" is that they may be forced— words and phrases injected into a moment or a person or a situation where they may not connect or even be clear. Sometimes Scripture is useful when you're sharing your faith, but sometimes it's not. Jesus looks at the moment: a well, a water jar, his thirst. He communicates. "You know, the stuff you're drinking probably leaves you thirsty, doesn't it?"

John's text says that this woman had been married several times. She had not found permanency in her life. Her several husbands (*ba'al* in Hebrew; also Ba'al, a deity) had not provided an answer to her search for meaning. Even that idolatry had not worked, nor had anything else. She was truly thirsty.

Jesus finds some language to say, "I know something that really satisfies. If you're interested, I'll tell you about it." Though the "living water" metaphor was present in the words of certain Hebrew prophets (Isaiah, Jeremiah, and Zechariah, for instance), I don't recall another time or place in the Gospels where Jesus talked to an individual about salvation as living water. He picks up a biblical metaphor and uses it here because it is the best way to communicate. His language is tailored to fit this situation.

Most people in today's society aren't thirsty for a lecture on theology, proofs for the existence of God, an explanation of the four theories of atonement, or a clarifying talk about the Trinity. As with this woman at the rest stop, their thirst is for hope and direction. If we listen to God, to the people we encounter, and to the moment of that encounter, I believe we can find fresh ways to share Christian faith as the answer to their needs.

Charles Colson discovered this when talking with an acquaintance who happened to be a prominent journalist. This man was intrigued by Colson's commitment to Christ, and they met for dinner to discuss it further. Colson came prepared with all sorts of arguments. But when he started talking about his experience with Christ, he was cut off. His friend told him it was wonderful that Colson had found peace and fulfillment, but that he did not believe in Jesus. He spoke of friends in the New Age movement who had found spirituality that worked for them as well as Christ worked for others. Colson then shifted gears and began to talk about eternal life. His friend had experienced serious health problems. Surely he had considered his own mortality. Again he was cut off. "Death is simply the end," his friend said. "When we die, we return to dust like trees or animals. No need to concern ourselves with an afterlife." Then Colson brought up the Bible, but the man refused to listen. "All legends," he said firmly.

Colson, the faith sharer, was at a loss for a moment. The man didn't care about God's plan for his life, about getting into heaven, or about the Bible. As Colson fumbled with his fork, an idea popped into his head. "Have you seen Woody Allen's

Crimes and Misdemeanors?" he asked. The man had, and they discussed the film for a few minutes. Then, catching him off guard, Colson asked, "Are you Judah Rosenthal?" His friend laughed nervously. Colson went on to say, "You may think this life is all there is but, if so, there's still an issue at hand. Namely, how do you live with yourself while you're here? I know you have a conscience, so how do you deal with that when you know you do wrong?"

The journalist admitted that this issue had given him a lot of problems. They moved into a discussion of Tolstoy's *War and Peace* and then of C. S. Lewis's concept of the natural law that is ingrained in all of us. That took them to the central point of Romans 1: that we are imbued with a conscience that points to questions that are answerable only outside of ourselves.

Colson ends the story by saying he doesn't know what's going to happen to his friend, but he has a hunch that through the work of the Holy Spirit he'll eventually come to Christ. He concludes that one thing is certain: without Woody Allen, Leo Tolstoy, and C. S. Lewis, he and his friend would not have found any common ground and language for a discussion of spiritual reality.[1] The best preparation for sharing your faith is prayer and a willingness to follow the leading of God's Spirit into the moments of encounter. That is how, I'm convinced, that Jesus did it at the rest stop—passing through Samaria and finding a way to communicate.

One other thing we can learn about faith sharing from this story is that *Jesus followed through.* This woman's life would not have been changed very much if Jesus had taken a drink of water, eaten some food, ended the conversation, and gotten back on the northbound road. His words would have been a warm and interesting memory, perhaps, but not much more. What happened instead is that Jesus and the disciples stopped and stayed two days in this Samaritan village, probably in somebody's home. What do you think happened during those two days? I think that Jesus spent them explaining, teaching, and helping this woman and her friends understand how the grace of God goes about changing a human life.

When it was time for Jesus to leave, the villagers said to the woman, "You were right. Now we've seen and heard for ourselves. Now we know that this is the Savior of the world." You have to decide that for yourself, of course—about his being *your* Savior—but you can best learn what that means in a fellowship where Jesus sticks around to teach you. *That's* why church matters: membership, commitment, participation. Whatever we do to lead people to the beginning step of faith, we must also lead them to the next necessary steps of fellowship and support. After all, the Great Commission mandate is about making disciples, not converts!

"Brother Turner," said the voice on the telephone, "I got saved on television last night, and I want to be baptized." I'll call him George. I knew him superficially. His family had started attending our church. He was a young man in his early twenties who had lost himself in the idolatries of alcohol, drugs, and sexual promiscuity. As we sat in my study the following week, he told me of having prayed "the sinner's prayer" during a Saturday night religious telecast. He felt better now—different—certain that he had been saved. As we talked about baptism, I was blunt and clear about baptism as an entry point to the church, the faith community that he would desperately need to help him understand and live out his new commitment. He listened patiently. He made promises about his involvement in the church. Shortly thereafter, he was baptized. After that, I saw him less and less. He would appear in a worship service now and then. I called, dropped by for visits, and talked with him at every opportunity about his need for us, his faith community, as he found his way into this new life of discipleship. Finally he dropped out completely and moved away.

I've seen that story repeated often enough in my years of pastoral ministry to understand that Jesus' decision to stay with this woman and her friends for a while is one of the most important parts of this story. He lingered only two or three days. It will certainly take us much longer to offer understanding and support to new believers. But his model is crystal clear. Jesus followed through.

Thinking back over this encounter from John's Gospel, I recall the story of Palmer Ofuoku, now a distinguished preacher in his native Nigeria. Although his family was not Christian, they sent him to a Christian mission school to get his education. There he remembers encountering many missionaries, some of whom clearly felt themselves superior to their African colleagues. One year a new missionary came to the school and began to invest himself emotionally in the lives of the Nigerians. He formed close, lasting relationships with many of them, including Palmer, whom he eventually led to faith in Jesus Christ. About that missionary Palmer Ofuoku said, "He built a bridge of friendship to me, and Jesus walked across."[2]

Being intentional—building bridges—listening to God's spirit in the moments and encounters of life—caring enough about people to hang around and follow through. There's a lot to be learned here about how Jesus shared his faith!

Notes

1. Charles Colson, *The Body* (Dallas: Word Publishing Company, 1992), pp. 336-38.

2. Palmer Ofuoku, cited by Michael Diduit, *Preaching* (March/April 1994): 49.

CHAPTER 3

With Someone
Who Had It Made

Luke 19:1-10

Presbyterian brother Charlie Shedd and I sat for a Sunday visit in my office one winter morning. He was doing a family life enrichment weekend in our church, and we were swapping stories between the two morning worship services. Charlie told an old story about a Texas pastor who decided he needed to do more personal evangelism, and so he set out in his car one afternoon to do precisely that. He came across a rancher surveying his field and cattle with one foot propped on the fence rail. The pastor said to himself, "I'm going to lead that man to faith." So he got out of his car and walked over to the fence. "Pardon me, sir, are you lost?" he began.

The rancher replied, "Why, no, I bought this ranch twenty-five years ago. I know every inch of it. I'm not lost."

"That's not what I mean," the pastor went on. "Are you a Christian?"

"No," said the rancher, "my name's Smith. The Christian spread is two spreads down. John and Hazel and their kids. They're good people, those Christians."

The pastor then said, "No, what I mean is, are you ready for the judgment?"

"When is it?" the rancher asked.

"Well, I don't know," the pastor said. "It could be tonight or it could be tomorrow night."

The rancher replied, "Well, don't tell my wife. She'll probably want to go both nights." Charlie and I laughed and agreed that clear communication is sometimes difficult!

When you're trying to share your Christian faith, it can't be prepackaged and cellophane-wrapped because you're standing at the corner of Gospel and specific personal need. At that intersection, need determines packaging, and Jesus himself is turning out to be our best example of this—with his family or with an unnamed Samaritan woman. Each context is different, so Jesus' approach is different. He understands that the kingdom of God grows a la Dean Witter: "one investor (or person) at a time." In his letters, C. S. Lewis says it's inevitable that we should be concerned about the salvation of those we know and love. "But we must be careful," he writes, "not to expect or demand that their salvation should conform to some ready-made pattern of our own."[1] Jesus takes context seriously. He takes people where he finds them. He listens to the moment. He shares his faith.

There were some who said no to Jesus' invitation to faith. But Zacchaeus, whom we meet in this chapter, said yes. Just before describing Jesus' encounter with Zacchaeus, Luke recalls a young man who said no to Jesus' invitation (Luke 18:18-30). Both individuals were persons of great wealth when Jesus met them. One chose life; the other did not. Jesus seems comfortable with letting people choose. A negative response does not change his feeling toward them. At other times, of course, the Gospel writers do not tell us how people decided or what happened after their decision. The New Testament is not a how-to manual on personal evangelism, but it does have stories that can teach us a lot. Consider the following one.

Jesus is going to Jerusalem, and Jericho is on the way—about fifteen miles away. In 1988 our tour bus stopped for lunch in

Jericho. We gazed down at the archeological evidence about the earliest walls, which collapsed before Joshua and the Israelites. We gazed up at a traditional site of Jesus' mountain of temptation. After lunch and on the way to Jerusalem, we rode over that narrow, snaking road between Jerusalem and Jericho where in Jesus' story a man fell among thieves and was left for dead. I have two photographs of that day that are memorable: one of Kelli sitting atop a camel and one of good friend Vernon Garrett climbing a tree in his hat and overcoat. It was January in Jericho, and we remembered Zacchaeus.

In this encounter Zacchaeus is called a "chief tax collector," the only usage of this phrase in the whole Bible or in Greek literature of the period. He is also called "rich." It was possible to be an honest tax collector, but you probably wouldn't be rich if you were. Most tax collectors cheated. They also had to deal with Rome and with pagan money (bearing idolatrous inscriptions of Caesar). Tax collectors frequented places that were ritually unclean and thus off-limits for devout Jews. Zacchaeus is deeply immersed in a corrupt system. As a chief tax collector, he may have been doubly rich, but he was also doubly despised by his fellow Jews of Jericho. Chief tax collector? "Chief of sinners" would have been more accurate in the eyes of the pious.

But Zack had what everybody seems to want—money, position, power. He is somebody who has it made. So why is he up in that tree? Well, he's rich, and rich people can do eccentric things. Or he's curious. Things can get pretty dull in Jericho when you're shut out and lonely. Or he does not want to miss the parade that is passing through his town. Or maybe he is up in that tree because he has it made but is running on empty and knows it. And here comes a rabbi who has been labeled a "friend of tax collectors and sinners." Zacchaeus, the man who had it made but did not have enough, did not want to miss this rabbi named Jesus. And Jesus didn't miss Zack!

Notice how Jesus shares his faith. *He stops.* Beginning in chapter 9 of his Gospel, Luke says that Jesus has his face "set to go to Jerusalem." Before he can get there, he heals lepers and a crippled woman and a man with dropsy. Before he gets to Jerusalem, he tells some of his best stories: the good Samaritan, the great dinner, the prodigal son, the rich man and Lazarus. Before he gets to Jerusalem, he stops along the way to help, to teach, to visit with children . . . and to share his faith. Jesus is just passing through Jericho, but he stops. Maybe because somebody here needs to know what Jesus is all about. It could have been anybody. It happened to be Zacchaeus.

Pause for a moment and consider the places you pass through. Who's there? Who's sitting at a desk? Standing at the copier? Living down the street? Making change at the service station? Checking you out at the supermarket? Taking a turn in the carpool? Showing up for Scouts or Little League? Is there somebody you need to stop for, pray for, speak to, establish a relationship with?

You can pass through people's lives again and again without ever stopping. Keith Miller recalls that after he had finished four terms at seminary, served on the vestries of two churches, and taught a large Sunday school class, a man who had worked with him in the same office for over a year said one day, "Gee, Keith, I didn't know you were a Christian." Miller was stunned to realize that although he had led Christ through every inner passage of his soul, he had obviously left him in the parking lot whenever he walked into his office.[2]

Is there somebody *you* need to stop for?

The statistics on unchurched Americans are crystal clear. About one out of every four would at least attend a church *if invited*, as the story of Sun Edwards proves. Sun Edwards serves with her husband, Fred, as a Baptist missionary to the International Seafarers Center near the port of Houston. Sun's family came to America in 1973 from their native Korea, and she and her brother were the first two Asians to attend their high school in Winchester, Virginia. Sun's father, Hyun Kuk Kim, had worked on American Army bases in Korea for a number of years, and viewing America as the land of opportunity, he migrated to this country. He got a job with a trucking company in Winchester, and in time brought his wife and three children to be with him.

Mr. Kim had a Buddhist background and was very cynical about Christianity. However, one day during the time he was living here alone, his foreman invited him to attend church. Surprisingly, he accepted that invitation, started attending, and within a few weeks had become a believer in Jesus Christ. When his family arrived from Korea, in traditional Korean fashion they all followed his lead in attending church. Over time, each of them became Christians.

Perhaps it was loneliness in a new land, curiosity about American Christianity, or the prayers of an older family member who was a Christian. Whatever factors were at work, the reality is that an *invitation* to Sunday worship with a Virginia Church of Christ congregation became a major step toward faith for the whole Kim family.

What people hear, feel, and experience when they worship is important, of course, but on any given Sunday, between fifteen and twenty million adults are sitting home, at least in part because no one ever extended an invitation. How many people is that? Try adding the populations of Houston, San Francisco, San Diego, Los Angeles, Detroit, Philadelphia, Chicago, and New York City. Put together, that's the size of our prospect pool among unchurched and uninvited Americans. Passing through Jericho, Jesus stops. Shouldn't we?

Next *Jesus speaks to the emptiness*. When Jesus came to the place, he looked up and said to him, "Zacchaeus, hurry and come down; for I must stay at your house today" (Luke 19:5). A rabbi under his roof? Maybe there's some hope here somewhere. Zacchaeus looks like one of those people who have been turned out or turned off by religious institutions. He's like 77 percent of all unchurched Americans. Churched as a child and perhaps an adolescent, he sang the songs, learned the language, and acquired a thin overlay of religion. But then his life took a different direction, and religion got left behind.

Unchurched Americans desert the church for various reasons. It may be the spotty history of organized religion—all the bad things that have been done in the name of God, from the Inquisition to religious intolerance to the local congregation that cannot resolve its conflicts in a healthy way. It may be the feeling that the church doesn't matter. In 1983, when Steve Jobs was building Apple Computer, he needed a world-class executive to take over the day-to-day affairs of his growing company. The question that he put to Pepsi-Cola executive John Sculley has passed into business history: "Do you want to spend the rest of your life selling sugared water, or do you want to change the world?"[3] An awful lot of unchurched Americans don't see the church as dealing with anything more important than sugared water—*not* changing the world and *not* making a difference in people's lives.

Or it may be due to unrealistic expectations. Being a Christian, they heard somewhere, brings guarantees that you won't get cancer, that your spouse won't leave, that your kids will turn out great, that your job will flourish. When things don't turn out that way, they leave.

In Zack's case it was his humanity that was not welcome in church. He was a human being who had worked very hard to get where he was. Sure, he trampled some values along the way and stiffed some people. So he was like anybody else—a human being, a sinner. Organized religion had no place for him. He might as well be dead. In fact, the Pharisees had a saying: "There is joy before God when those who provoke him perish from the world."

So here's Zacchaeus, turned off and tuned out, with this hole in his heart, and Jesus speaks to that emptiness. "I'll go home with you. I'll spend some time with you. *I'll be your friend.*" Zack could understand that. It was crystal clear good news.

Unlike Jericho, the city in which I live and work is huge. We're more than four million strong and scattered across five hundred square miles. Yet my town is composed of individuals like Zacchaeus. I meet them often. What they say to me verbally and nonverbally is, "I'll be just fine if I can work a little harder, eat less fat, work out more regularly, drink better Scotch, or find a younger sex partner."

Some of them get it—money and power and position. But after a while, and especially as they get older, it seems hollow. Texan Bob Buford remembers a remark made by a Harvard-educated businessman. Recalling many successes in his chosen field, the man said, "I was always finding out that beyond the pot of gold at the end of the rainbow, there's a sort of emptiness."[4]

In their recent book, *The Search for Meaning,* Naylor, Willimon, and Naylor point out that pure American consumerism is not all it's cracked up to be. In public opinion polls since 1957, the percentage of Americans claiming to be "very happy" has remained fixed at about 33 percent, while personal consumption has doubled![5] Obviously, the emptiness of acquisition and control is real among us. Like Jesus, we can speak to that emptiness in a plain and straightforward way. "I'll spend some time with you. I'll care about you. I'll help you find what you did not find in faith before."

When Jesus does this, the religious establishment mutters, "This fits what we've heard about him, how fast and loose he plays with the rules of piety." It wasn't true, of course, but they were into rules and rituals and propping up religious institutions. Jesus was into finding people's emptiness and trying to address it. Shouldn't we be doing that?

One other thing about this encounter is that *Jesus offers a relationship.* "Zacchaeus," says Jesus, "I must stay at your house today." Did he stay there? For how long? The text is somewhat unclear. It says that Zack "hurried down and welcomed him." Onlookers said, "He's gone to be a guest in a sinner's home." Jesus said, "Salvation has come to this house." Verse 8 of the story just says that Zacchaeus stood and made his profession of faith: "Four hundred percent restitution for what I have stolen and one-half of everything to the poor."

However long or short his encounter with Jesus, Zack understands that there is an unbreakable connection between faith and lifestyle. Maybe he knew it instantly, recalling something from his boyhood sabbath school lessons. But now, faced with Jesus, faced with the exciting and demanding possibilities of living in a different way, I think he might have needed a day or so with Jesus or a friendship with some other disciples. Somebody helped him work it out . . . to really see how faith gets lived out in difficult and daily choices. That takes time, and it takes the committed friendship of others who travel the faith journey with us.

Zacchaeus reminds me of a young church member I know who dropped out of active church life during his years in the military. Returning to the States with a wife and two young children, he found his way to our church and along with his family began to worship with us. After he had joined our fellowship, he said to me one day, "Bill, this church has been great for me. Several years ago I threw out a lot of baggage. I now know a lot of the things about organized religion that I no longer need or accept. What I have found here among these people is a place to decide what I *do* believe and how it really works day-to-day."

Most unchurched Americans do not know the connection between faith and daily life—including their business ethics, their family relationships, their sexual choices, their use of money and time. How will they learn? From somebody who offers a relationship, somebody who points the way from conversion to discipleship, somebody who cares enough to build long-range relationships.

In 1964 the editorial page of the *Chicago Daily News* carried the story of Jerry Hollins, a twenty-five-year-old African American from Louisiana who came to Chicago looking for a better life. After two years in the city, he had not found much work. He started hanging around the bus station. When a policeman asked

him why he was loitering there, he did not have a good answer
and was arrested for disorderly conduct. The judge set his fine
at one hundred dollars. He didn't have any money, so he worked
off the fine in the laundry of the House of Corrections. He listed
no relatives, and nobody came to see him. On the day of his
release, he crawled out on a ledge in the U.S. Courthouse
rotunda, seven stories above the lobby floor. It took him so long
to work up his nerve that firemen were able to get there with a
net; it broke his fall when he finally jumped. He suffered a broken
pelvis, a collapsed lung, broken ribs, and other serious injuries.
Just before he jumped, a minister caught Hollins's attention and
said, "Don't jump, son. God loves you." Jerry Hollins yelled,
"What God?" Then he jumped.[6]

Words are never enough in sharing our faith. If words are all
we have to offer, they will be swallowed up by the competing
noises of modern life. The truly unique gifts we have to give are
the ones that Jesus gave to Zacchaeus: friendship, time, acceptance. Zacchaeus discovered the answer to Jerry Hollins's question through a relationship with a very human being who passed
through Jericho and stopped for him.

Zacchaeus is a "son of Abraham," but he has lost his way. Then
and now, he is rich and he is powerful, but he is empty. He has
turned away from religion, but Jesus' friendship shows him that
there's more to faith than what he rejected.

About this encounter with Zacchaeus, Jesus said, "The son of
man came to seek out and save the lost." Shouldn't *we* be saying,
offering, and doing something like that?

Notes

1. W. H. Lewis, ed., *Letters of C. S. Lewis* (New York: Harcourt
Brace Jovanovich, 1966), p. 261.

2. Keith Miller, *The Taste of New Wine* (Waco, Tex.: Word, 1968),
p. 79.

3. Roy O'Connor, "Apple Chief Sculley Finally Making the Company His Own," *Chicago Tribune*, 1 June 1991, sec. 4, p. 1.

4. Bob Buford, *Halftime* (Grand Rapids: Zondervan, 1994), p. 86.

5. Thomas H. Naylor, William H. Willimon, Magdalena R. Naylor, *The Search for Meaning* (Nashville: Abingdon, 1994), p. 90.

6. Carroll Wise, *The Meaning of Pastoral Care* (New York: Harper and Row, 1966), p. 16.

CHAPTER 4

With Someone
Ready to Give Up

Matthew 9:18-26

By the time Mark (most likely the earliest of our four Gospels) was written, three decades or more had passed since the actual events of Jesus' life had taken place—thirty years plus. Stop for a moment and think about how long that is. Some of us have not even lived that long, but if you have, try to think back to what was happening in your world thirty years ago today. What do you remember now about then, and why do you remember it?

These are the kinds of issues that the writers and editors of Mark, Matthew, Luke, and John had to face. Of course they had spoken as well as written stories, all circulating in the New Testament church. Soon it was time to collect and organize their data. Christ had not returned, and the generation that had witnessed the events and the stories was dying out. Clearly the church needed to act to preserve its history. But what to include? And what to leave out?

Several factors helped answer such questions, one of which was the shape of the church itself thirty years or more after Jesus. It was filling up with all kinds of people. Gentiles were coming in and would soon outnumber Jews. People in distant places to which the gospel had spread were also coming in—people who once had worshiped all kinds of other gods or no gods at all. Slaves who had never been free physically or politically were experiencing spiritual freedom. People were coming from the ranks of the rejected and despised classes—women, children, the poor, and various other outcasts. Thus one struggle that the early church faced was whether to maintain an open-door policy toward absolutely everybody.

My personal conviction is that the Gospel writers chose some of their written material to answer just that question. Based on the evidence that they preserved for us, it is quite clear that the Lord of the church was inclusive in his love and acceptance of people. The Gospel accounts show us Jesus sharing his faith with various people, including his family, who were unsure about him for a long time. There were divided families in the early church. Some family members believed; some did not. In welcoming Zacchaeus, Jesus shows how to welcome a despised one into the fellowship of faith. The church needed that model. When Jesus and the disciples spend a couple of days with the Samaritan woman and her village, we get a clear picture of his reaching out to races and nationalities different from his own. The church really needed that model. Thus I am suggesting that the early church learned about outreach and inclusion from Jesus. His example directed both their writing and their witnessing.

Years ago, when theologian Howard Thurman was a guest preacher in India, there came a tap at his door late one evening. He opened the door to find a young Indian boy standing timidly before him. Working up his nerve, he blurted out, "I stood outside the window tonight and heard you preach. Tell me, have you got any hope for a nobody?" Before Thurman could answer, the young man's courage faded, and he dashed off into the bushes.[1] The materials included in the Gospel accounts strongly suggest that the earliest believers were struggling hard to treat everybody as a *somebody* within reach of God's grace.

In the encounter now before us, we meet two females: a child, who is dead or dying when her desperate father comes to Jesus, and an adult, who desperately lunges forward to touch him. Remember that women ranked just above slaves and children in the social and cultural pecking order of Jesus' day. The fact that he would stop what he was doing and give attention to these two females may have been significant to the early church, since all three Gospels include this story.

There are some people here who are ready to give up. The father—Mark and Luke call him Jairus—is a lay leader in the local synagogue. He's important, he's respected, he's religious. But today he's just Daddy, and he's at the end of his rope. The descriptions in Mark and Luke are especially poignant. They tell us that the little girl is an only daughter and that she is twelve years old. (Today at that age a Jewish girl comes into woman-hood—her bat mitzvah year.) She has been loved and nurtured for twelve years, and now death has struck her down. After nearly four decades of pastoral ministry, I can tell you that the death of a child—at any age—is probably the hardest loss in life. I have watched sixty-year-old parents who have lost a forty-year-old child grieve just as profoundly as parents who lose newborns, preteens, or adolescents. Nothing makes life seem more out of control than the death of a child.

But Jesus is not helpless before this ancient enemy. He raises this child back to life, as he later does Lazarus (John 11:38-44) and the widow's son (Luke 7:11-17). All of them, like all of us, would ultimately die, but not here and not now. In this moment Jesus' power triumphs over death. Easter is the great and culmi-nating sign of God's triumph over the grave. Still, death finds all of us at the end of our human, medical, and secular ropes. "Lord, come . . . Lord, help" is an honest cry for aid in this devastating human experience. Jairus does not fully understand Jesus or his message, but he is a seeker after hope. He is someone open to whatever help Jesus has to offer in this tragic hour.

Remember this about unchurched Americans. One of the times we see them in church is when somebody dies. That is one of the best chances I have as a pastor to share my faith. In an

afternoon pastors' dialogue four years ago, James Forbes, pastor
of New York City's Riverside Church, commented to us that his
funeral preaching was probably his most significant preaching.
That squares with what I have experienced as well. A memorial
service can be a bottom-line, no-nonsense time in people's lives.
The death of another confronts me with my own mortality. It
poses ageless and troubling questions, such as, What am I doing
with my life? Does it matter that I am living? Is the hope of life
after death an honest option for me?

In my files I have a now yellowed clipping from *USA Today.*
Michael Levine is a Los Angeles writer and public relations
executive whose op-ed piece I read on a 1993 airline flight.
Levine writes that if he could ever be "king of America," his first
act would be to require every person under forty to attend a
funeral service once a year. He came to this conclusion after
attending the funeral of a friend's father, where the speakers
talked about the man's relationships with family and friends, but
made no mention at all of his professional or business accom-
plishments. There was an amazing contrast, he says, between
dedication to things like hard work and career advancement and
the reality that we will probably be remembered for how we
connected with other humans emotionally and spiritually. A
slogan popular in the late 1980s, Whoever dies with the most
toys, wins, lost its appeal for Levine on the day of that funeral.
Levine concluded that if young people spent at least an hour a
year listening to what people are remembered for, it might point
their lives in a new direction.

Levine's piece tells me nothing about his personal religious
convictions, but it sends a clear signal that a memorial service
can be a teachable moment. Sometimes, as with Jairus, Jesus is
welcomed into those sad and desperate moments—along with
an openness to his word that has not existed before.

But there is another person in our story—a woman who
(unlike the man, Jairus) does not approach Jesus directly. She is
also ready to give up, having tried everything to escape her

disease. Mark says that she suffered under many doctors. (Luke, who is a doctor, leaves that out.) But all accounts portray her as hopeless and desperate. She is physically sick and weak. She is a social outcast. (The law said she could not be allowed into the temple.) She is religiously suspect, since the popular understanding of the time was that sickness was usually the result of some sin. This woman with her chronic hemorrhage must have looked like a great sinner to others. Finally, she is a woman. (The leper in Matthew 8 comes directly to Jesus, but then he's a man.)

The woman does a strange thing. An exile from human touch for twelve long years, she now gropes and grabs for the corner of Jesus' robe as he passes by. And Jesus does an even stranger thing. He stops and turns. Seeing her, he talks with her—and she is made whole. The gospel is not just for the well bred and the well behaved; it is for the desperate and the downtrodden as well.

How does Jesus share his faith in this situation? For one thing, *he becomes part of her life process*. In this story, as in others, the Gospel writer gives us a small snippet of the person's encounter with Jesus. The brief description makes this life-changing moment seem sudden and brief. What we do not see is the life process that led to the moment of encounter.

Any experience of spiritual rebirth is preceded by months or years of incubation. In 1977, while the Trans-Alaska Pipeline was being built, a young man named David Enroth came to Houston to call on some of the oil companies in our city. He was in town for only a week or so, but one night he met Sue Olds in his hotel lobby. They struck up a conversation, and she encouraged him to join her for worship in South Main Baptist Church the following Sunday. He attended the morning and evening services, and has not been back since. He and Sue saw each other face-to-face a total of three times. Nearly twenty years after their first meeting, in the spring of 1996, David was baptized into the fellowship of the First Baptist Church in Seattle, Washington. His fax to me celebrating his decision about faith and church membership reads, "experienced a spiritual holocaust as a child that separated me from God for a while. In 1977, I met Sue Olds in Houston, Texas. Sue introduced me to South Main Baptist Church. South Main is the church that, by its example, returned me to a personal spiritual quest. Following my father's death on April 7, 1995, I experienced a spiritual awakening and rebirth."

David's life process included a childhood that was marred by disillusionment about faith, marriage to a loving Buddhist wife, Sue Olds, South Main Baptist Church, the Presbyterian pastor who conducted his father's memorial service, Rod Romney, pastor of Seattle's First Baptist Church, and many others. His choice of Christian faith came at the end of a lengthy season of preparation. Now, joyfully, the choice had been made. David described it to me in these words: "I have been liberated; I have found a way. I love and accept God, as I am loved and accepted by the Eternal One."

You may be the person who is actually on the scene when the faith commitment is made, or you may be person number six or person number twenty-four along the way. Wherever you fall in their life process, don't discount it! In terms of "church growth" and numerical increases, it is vital to remember that not everything that counts can be counted. Nearly 80 percent of people who become Christians do so because of encouragement from someone they trust. You could be someone who is there when Jesus passes by or someone who prepares a person for a later time when Jesus passes by.

I once heard American business guru Ken Blanchard tell about his friendship with Jan Carlzon, CEO of Scandinavian Airlines. The company was on the verge of collapse when Carlzon became its president, and he decided to institute a program of people-first, user-friendly service. It helped tremendously, and Scandinavian is now one of the most successful airlines in the business. Blanchard remembered standing at a Scandinavian counter with a ticket mix-up. The airport was crowded, and the counter was busy, and it would have been easy for the young woman at the counter to say, "Sorry, you'll just have to wait. There is nothing

I can do right now." Instead, she pointed him in the right direction, called ahead, and even accompanied him part of the way to make sure that he got the right connecting flight. After the incident Blanchard wrote Carlzon to compliment this young employee. "It was," he said, "a moment of truth about Carlzon's company." That's the phrase, incidentally, that Carlzon uses with his employees—moment of truth. It's that moment when people form an impression of an organization based on the care and service they receive in a particular situation. All of the advertising, promotion, and reputation of a company or institution aren't nearly as effective as how people experience it when *their* lives and needs are on the line.

Implications for the church? They're obvious, aren't they? Images on a billboard or a bumper sticker, pictures on a television screen, or words in a newspaper ad may get someone's attention for an instant. Such "marketing" may build up institutional awareness. But it is the times of pain, loneliness, grief, celebration, uncertainty, or transition that can be "moments of truth" about us to neighbors and friends who are passing through such times. Effective evangelism is more than telling—it's always showing and telling. Entering the life process of another person may happen unexpectedly and suddenly during the crisis situations of life. However, our care and trustworthiness as bearers of God's grace can also be established in the process of day-to-day relationships.

I learned this afresh one busy day, listening across the lunch table to a young man describe his personal and marital struggles. My schedule that day was tight, my mind preoccupied, my attention divided. About fifteen minutes into lunch, however, my young friend corrected my priorities. "This time means a lot to me," he said, "because there aren't that many people who think I'm important." I woke up at that point, and a routine lunch became a moment of truth about me and my faith community.

At South Main Baptist Church in Houston, we don't have evening worship on fifth Sunday nights. Instead, we encourage our people, who live scattered throughout the city, to host or cohost gatherings called "South Main in My Neighborhood." We have found that "having folks over" is a way to begin cultivating friendships and building bridges. Houston is a huge city with a crime problem. A lot of us live behind burglar bars, fences, air conditioning, and alarm systems. We may go for years barely knowing our neighbors by name, let alone their family situations, spiritual needs, or life processes. South Main in My Neighborhood is helping us break through some of these barriers. Besides those who live on our street, our neighbors are people in the workplace, in Little League, in the P.T.A., in civic clubs. We encourage our people to keep preparations for these gatherings simple—sandwiches, coffee, dessert. They do not pass out church literature, play a videotape of the morning worship service, or invite the pastor to drop by. What we're trying to do is to build relationships now so that when opportunities and teachable moments come later, our personal witness will have the integrity of a personal relationship. "Networking" has long been one of the most commonly used practices in American business. This simple program is proving useful as a neighbor network that discovers unchurched Houstonians. It's not a hard sell or a quick sell of the gospel. Rather, it's an opportunity for the intentional cultivation of persons with whom we have a superficial acquaintance.

Ours is a busy church with a wide variety of ministries and programs. Our members spend a lot of time on the South Main campus and in contact with other believers. There is nothing wrong with these activities, but they do not necessarily bring us into contact with unchurched people. We have to be intentional about that, so we have designed this Sunday night schedule with that as our goal. It's too early to tell what the results will be, since cultivation evangelism is a long-term process. Personally, I think this ministry of friendship is going to be a significant one for our people. As the warm hospitality of our church gets multiplied around the city over time and works its way into the life process of our friends and neighbors, it's sure to make an impact. Look at any of the reasons why people come to a church, for example, location, advertising, music, preaching, program. Taken together, they account for perhaps 10 percent of the newcomers. Between 80 and 90 percent of people, however, are drawn to a church by the cultivation and invitation of persons *other than* pastor or staff member. They apparently are more apt to listen to someone who shares their daily turf than to a paid professional.

Establishing relationships within the normal frameworks of life, nurturing those relationships, inviting and welcoming people on the basis of those relationships most certainly makes a difference, but we must be intentional about doing it. There are no shortcuts or substitutes. Management expert Peter Drucker is on target when he reminds us that strategy is worthless until it degenerates into work!

Eight-year-old Rachel McCarty is a good model. When her family moved to a new house last year, she got out her colored chalk and on the sidewalk in front of her house wrote, "I am new here. I want to be your friend. Please come play with me." Then she drew big arrows leading from the sidewalk to the front door and added under each arrow, "Don't be afraid. Don't be afraid. Don't be afraid." Her grandmother called that "reaching out in bright colors." For neighborhood networking, Rachel has the right idea!

There's something else about Jesus in this story. We've seen it before. He shares his faith *during an interruption*. He obviously has a teaching agenda during this part of his ministry. The text says, "Suddenly, a leader of the synagogue" comes into his life and "suddenly, a woman" approaches. Jesus made choices. He "went with" Jairus. He "turned and saw" this woman. You can't live your life bouncing off interruptions and responding to the agendas of other people, but there are times when God is at work in those interruptions. One of the clear implications of Jesus' story of the good Samaritan is that while a priest and a Levite were on their way to do God's work in the temple, they failed to see God's presence in the ditch by the side of the road, in a battered body, and in a bothersome interruption. But how do you know when to stop and pay attention to the interruptions?

I think the key, again, is in the model of Jesus. Nobody lived a busier life than he did, but he always found time for prayer. More than anything else, prayer kept him in touch with God in the interruptions of life. Knowing God well enough in the quiet place helped him recognize God in the marketplace. Sharing your faith is not all up to you! God is your partner, and the Holy Spirit works in people's lives to prepare them. Trust that as solid truth, and pray daily for God's direction.

I often wake up early, and I like to pray through what I know about the day's schedule as I lie in bed at that early hour. I see the faces connected with my appointments and commitments. Some of those people I have been able to share my faith with. Usually the day brings with it surprises, interruptions, and persons who need some warmth and caring from me. Sometimes I am tempted to rush right past them. But I am convinced that my early morning prayers have actually sensitized me to God's presence at the feverish intersections of daily life.

Remember that times of crisis and transition—especially the painful ones—are times when people reach out. For Jairus, it was a child's terminal illness. For an unnamed woman, it was a chronic hemorrhage. Death, illness, marital separation, job loss, retirement, changes in residence, marital reconciliation, birth or adoption, graduation from school—all are times when people may reach out, groping for God. For these people in transition, you and I are not able to do all that Jesus does, but we can pay attention to how God may be at work in the interruptions in their lives—and in how they interrupt ours!

Jesus also shared his faith in this encounter *by listening*. Mark's Gospel says that when Jesus stopped, the woman told him her whole story. Everybody has a story, even someone who is ready to give up. Listening is a way of saying, "I care about you." God gave us two ears and one mouth, maybe for a very good reason! Christian witness is *not* all talk. Listening lets you learn what lies beneath the surface of the story. I suspect that this woman felt about as much shame and guilt as she did physical discomfort. Usually the surface story is *not* the whole story, so we need to listen.

A young woman sat across the desk from me in a Kentucky church. The story on the table was about her marriage—the abuse and conflict that she was enduring. As we talked, I asked, "Helen, how do you feel about being a wife and a mother?" I'll never forget her dropped head, fidgeting fingers, and mumbled response. "I don't know why anybody would like me," she said. That was her deeper story, and we started to work with it through baptism and new friendships and the worth-bestowing love of a church family. The dynamics of her troubled marriage were significant, and one of them turned out to be her own lack of self-worth. I learned that by listening.

Sometimes listening lets you hear the spiritual baggage that burdens people as well. In our biblical story the woman's faith was probably a mixture of faith and superstition. "If I just touch his garment, I'll be healed." Flawed assumptions and unrealistic expectations are often a part of their stories. Faith that is flawed or simplistic or superstitious can be unlearned. First, however, it needs to be heard and understood. Jesus listens to the woman's story, and he does not penalize her for misunderstandings in it.

One Sunday morning, a man walked into our worship service and sat down. He listened to the sermon and came down the aisle during the invitation hymn. I had never seen him before. He said, "I want to be saved. I want God to forgive me." Later that week we sat in my study, and I asked him to tell me more about his decision to join our church. I discovered that ours wasn't the only church he had joined. The count was four or five over recent weeks. "Why?" I asked. "I just want to be sure I'm saved," he said. "Sure that I'm OK with God." We talked further. When I asked him about his family and childhood, he told me about his father. "No matter what I did," he said, "it wasn't enough to please my father. When I disobeyed, I was whipped and whipped and whipped. Then he would never let us kids forget what we had done wrong." Most of us come to God with a flawed faith. This man was frantically searching for assurance of God's love and forgiveness, and we started to work on the story *behind* his story.

Jesus listens, and we can too. What is the pain? Where is it coming from? What are the assumptions? How is faith understood and described? What is the searcher actually looking for? Swiss doctor Paul Tournier says that to live meaningfully, each of us must be understood by at least one other human being. I believe that people search for that understanding in many places, including marriage, friendship, work relationships, drugs, promiscuity, and the neighborhood bar. If you and I can be listeners—understanding listeners—we will be able to help. We will also find opportunities to share our faith.

One last thing about the "hem of his garment." In Numbers 15 there is an instruction to wear tassels on the corners of your robe as reminders to obey the commandments of God, not the commandments of lust. These fringes were the mark of a devout person in Jesus' day and are still found on Jewish prayer shawls. Jesus looked beyond those tassels to see the people wearing them because people are what God's commandments are mostly about.

Are there religious and institutional "tassels" that we need to see beyond? Worship attendance, Bible study, tithing, and Christian fellowship are all worthy expressions of obedience to God. They may also be measurable marks of our devotion. But seeing, listening, and cultivating relationships with those outside of faith was one of the priorities of Jesus' lifetime. *He* looked beyond the tassels! Isn't there a message in this for *us*?

Note

1. Gene Bartlett, *Postscript to Preaching* (Valley Forge, Pa.: Judson, 1981), p. 69.

Chapter 5

With a Leader Who Lost His Way

John 3:1-10

Here's how Frederick Buechner sees it:

Nicodemus has heard enough about what Jesus was up to in Jerusalem to make him think he ought to pay him a visit and find out more. On the other hand, as a VIP with a big theological reputation to uphold, he decided it might be just as well to pay it at night. Better to be at least fairly safe than to be sorry, he thought, and waited till he thought his neighbors were all asleep.

So Nicodemus was fairly safe, and, at least at the start of their nocturnal interview, Jesus was fairly patient. What the whole thing boiled down to, Jesus told him, was that unless you got born again, you might as well give up.

That was all very well, Nicodemus said, but just how were you supposed to pull a thing like that off? How especially were you supposed to pull it off if you were pushing sixty-five? How did you get born again when it was a challenge just to get out of bed in the morning? He even got a little sarcastic. Could a man "enter a second time into his mother's womb," he asked, when it was all he could do to enter a taxi without the driver's coming around to give him a shove from behind?

A gust of wind happened to whistle down the chimney at that point, making the dying embers burst into flame, and Jesus said being born again was like that. It wasn't something you did. The wind did it. The Spirit did it. It was something that happened, for God's sake.

"How can this be?" Nicodemus said, and that's when Jesus let him have it.

Maybe Nicodemus had six honorary doctorates and half a column in Who's Who, Jesus said, but if he couldn't see something as plain as the nose on his face, he'd better go back to kindergarten.

"I'm telling you like it is," Jesus said, "I'm telling you what I've seen. I'm telling you there are people on Medicare walking around with the love-light in their eyes. I'm telling you there are ex-cons teaching Sunday School. I'm telling you there are undertakers scared silly we'll put them out of business."

Jesus said, "I'm telling you God's got such a thing for this loused-up planet that he's sent me down so if you don't believe your own eyes, then maybe you'll believe mine, maybe you'll believe me, maybe you won't come sneaking around scared half to death in the dark any more but will come to, come clean, come to life."

What impressed Nicodemus even more than the speech was the quickening of his own breathing and the pounding of his own heart. He hadn't felt like that since his first pair of long pants, his first kiss, since the time his first child was born or the time they'd told him he didn't have lung cancer but just a touch of flu.

Later on, when Jesus was dead, he went along with Joseph of Arimathea to pay his last respects at the tomb in broad daylight. It was a crazy thing to do, what with the witch-hunt that was going on, but he decided it was more than worth it.

When he heard the next day that some of the disciples had seen Jesus alive again, he wept like a newborn baby.[1]

I think that Buechner really does capture the flavor of this particular encounter. Nicodemus is a pivotal New Testament character because he is so much like so many of the people in

Jesus' world—moral, religious, well-intentioned. He seeks out Jesus, has this conversation, and goes away. He reappears twice in John's Gospel (and nowhere else): once in chapter 7, when he advises the other Pharisees to give Jesus a fair hearing, and once in chapter 19, when he brings ointment so that Jesus' body can be given a decent burial.

But John's Gospel never quite says that he became a believer. Joseph of Arimathaea, who helped him bury Jesus' body, is called "a secret disciple." But the text does not actually say that about Nicodemus. Even Jesus, who shares his faith with Nicodemus, can't guarantee what the result of that faith sharing will be.

We put a lot of pressure on ourselves when we think that this witnessing business has to work. If we would give up that notion, that witnessing *has to work,* we would probably find sharing our faith a lot easier. Every faith-sharing situation involves the work of God's Spirit, the circumstances of the moment, the baggage of personal history, and whatever verbal contribution we make. There is also the autonomy of an individual who is free to say no, yes, maybe, or in a while. We have to trust the process, believing that God is actively involved in it. It also helps to remember that God has many resources besides us!

In his encounter with Nicodemus, *Jesus starts by redefining reality.* At the outset, Jesus does not seem to be listening to Nicodemus. Nicodemus says, "We (all of us Pharisees and religious leaders) know that God is with you." And Jesus says, "The kingdom of God is not what you folks think it is." How does that fit? Are they talking past each other?

Not for long. "If God is with me," Jesus is saying, "then God is doing a brand-new thing. Nicodemus, reality is shifting." Here is present reality for Nicodemus. He is a Pharisee, a member of the most highly regarded religious brotherhood of his time. He is a member of the Sanhedrin, the council of elders for the nation. He is a teacher of the law—a trained theologian. Jesus does not deprecate any of this. He just says that it is not what's real spiritually. Nicodemus has lived his life by the book, but somewhere along the way his crowd has lost its way to a meaningful relationship with God. Nicodemus has followed the formulas and the traditions well. Here he is, at the top of his game, and Jesus talks about something he missed—something that can only come "from above."

"Success," said Emilie Griffin, "disappoints us because we had so thoroughly expected it to be the crown of life."[2] Nicodemus had made it to the top in religion by the book. Other people make it in business, or in a profession, or in school, or in social status. But everybody gets the same message about reality. "If you jump through these hoops, play by these rules, success will come. Then life will be what it's supposed to be."

What we discover instead is that success is less satisfying than we thought it would be. After winning the prestigious Wimbledon Tournament, a champion tennis player commented, "The thrill of victory lasts about fifteen minutes."[3] No reality is as exciting as the dream we had of it.

I have a colleague who has served some of the larger churches in our denomination. I once heard him tell a story about when he was a ministerial student in a Baptist college, sitting in a Sunday worship service and listening to a sermon by the highly regarded pastor. "I remember thinking to myself," he said, "that if I could ever do that, it would be the ultimate success of my life." Interestingly enough, years later he was called to the pastorate of that large church. "I can tell you now," he said, "it wasn't nearly as great as I thought it would be. There isn't any place or any ministry that is big enough to satisfy all our needs."

There's no pulpit, no front-office desk, no business or professional platform that serves as the ultimate reality. "Nicodemus, you've made it, but it's an empty reality. What God actually made you for is from above, and until you let *that* wind blow and keep on blowing through your life, you'll keep on struggling to find something real." An awful lot of unchurched Americans are right there with Nicodemus.

Present reality, whatever it is for them, just is not working.

The good news is that some of them already suspect that the deeper, better reality is spiritual in nature. It has been a long time since Edna St. Vincent Millay wrote her poem about the death of God, but it still describes the spiritual hunger of many a life. In "Conversation at Midnight," she says, "Man has never been the same since God died." We laugh louder, drink longer, fidget more, and we do it all in broad daylight. But "as soon as it is night," says the poet, we "go out and howl over the grave of God." Indeed, if all the promises of modernism and technology and success are turning up empty, there's something to howl about.

One thing we can do for successful people like Nicodemus is help them redefine reality. Is this all there is, and is it enough? Do your motivations give you lasting purpose? Are you at peace? Are you busy doing good things but feeling empty inside? Is there a craving in your life that your success has not satisfied? Like Nicodemus, some of these folks are involved in religious activities, church membership, or good causes. Without the inwardness of a personal relationship with God, however, they are running on empty, and many are burning out.

Since most people find dealing with such issues difficult and since they may not be ready to even consider a different look at reality, notice a second strategy Jesus uses with Nicodemus: *he starts a relationship.* As we mentioned earlier, the New Testament refers to Nicodemus in only two other places. The story in John 3 is the longest New Testament description of an encounter between Jesus and a named person, but there is no way of knowing whether or not he spends significant time with Jesus again. What Jesus says to him here, however, offers him an open door. "Don't be surprised that I'm telling you that you need to be born again—from above." But Nicodemus is surprised, as well as confused and trapped, in his system for success. Jesus talks about a relationship with God and likens it to the wind. It's more mystery than answers. God comes more in glimpses than full portrait. But this means that faith is not frozen; it's fresh and open-ended. That, says Jesus to Nicodemus, is the way to really live.

Six times in these ten verses, Nicodemus uses the verb *can.* "*Can* it happen?" "How *can* anyone?" "How *can* these things be?" In his well-chosen, well-frozen state of mind, it all sounds too complicated—or too simple. So Nicodemus is struggling to know if the new reality Jesus offers is actually possible for him. Maybe this fresh new understanding is the way to go, but he has questions, doubts, and excuses.

I don't think Nicodemus decides anything at this moment except to think about what he has heard and felt in this encounter. He needs time to weigh it, and perhaps he will ask for more time with Jesus to discuss it. There's no way to know, of course, if he and Jesus actually spent that additional time, but my guess is that if they did not, Nicodemus did not become a believer. Possibly after Jesus' resurrection, but who knows? The point here is that Jesus opens the door and starts a relationship.

We can do that too. We can establish ongoing relationships with "successful" unchurched people. To busy, hard-driving individuals, we can offer our time. Most of them know the value and the scarcity of it, and there's nothing we could offer that would say "love" more clearly to them. During that time and in that relationship we can share information, clarification, understanding, and encouragement. A pastor invited a young executive to a church Bible study group. "Would I learn about that John 3:16 thing in the group?" he asked. When a puzzled look spread over the pastor's face, the young man continued: "You know, that John 3:16 I see on TV sports events all the time."[4]

There is, out there in America, a lot of superficial awareness and natural curiosity about spiritual things. Many people carry baggage from their encounters with organized religion. Like Nicodemus, they need someone who will over time help them unpack it, look at it, keep it, discard it, or change it.

There's one more thing that makes starting a relationship so important in faith sharing. How people get to their point of commitment to Christ has a lot to do with their expectations about Christian discipleship *and* with what happens to them after they have decided for Christ and faith.

Win Arn, who once worked with the Billy Graham organization, now does research for an organization that tracks church growth. He groups outreach methods into three main categories. First, there's what he calls *information transmission*. Christian witness here is verbally communicating facts and propositions. The assumption is that the hearer who understands correctly the information that is being transmitted will give mental assent to those facts and make a decision for Christ. Arn's research revealed that 75 percent of those approached in this way will say no to the invitation to discipleship. A second category he calls *manipulative monologue*. This may be an emotional appeal, or it may be some carefully prepared questions to which the hearer can only give yes answers. This is a classic sales pitch, and the goal is to close the sale. Follow-up shows that while 81 percent of those approached in this way may make a decision for Christ, within a year's time, 85 percent of them will drop out of church. The third category Arn calls *nonmanipulative dialogue*. Here the assumption is that no "canned" approach is appropriate in every situation, since people are unique. Thus the relationship between the witness and the unchurched person is the critical factor. The goal is a longer-term relationship in which friendship, love, and faith may be shared and understood. Arn found that 99 percent of these people eventually decide for Christ, and 96 percent of them become active in the church.[5]

Christian faith grows best in an extended relationship. Information is shared, questions are answered, sin and repentance get clarified. All of this happens best in the context of an extended relationship of friendship and trust. Jesus' invitation, "Follow me!" is quoted more than thirty times in the Gospels. The term *born again from above* is used just once. This may be significant!

In Nicodemus Jesus met a person who needed to think about reality as he was experiencing it. What Jesus said to Nicodemus in his first encounter with him would need clarification and fresh understanding later. My personal conviction about this story is that Jesus opened a relationship with Nicodemus and invited him to follow.

David Allen was one of the first African Americans on the faculty of the Harvard medical school. In the early 1970s he was asked to mediate racial tension that had erupted in Roxbury. As he walked through the area seeing apartments burning and stores being looted, he said to himself, "I wish Jesus were here today. He could resolve this." Then from somewhere inside a voice said, "But I am. Only now I live in you and through you." Allen reports that was one of his life's most teachable moments, handing him an insight that continues to influence all of his work.[6] I believe that Jesus wants to share faith with the Nicodemuses of our time *through us*.

Pioneer missionary David Livingston walked the continent of Africa, sharing the gospel of Christ through personal engagement and caring in a thousand villages over a period of several years. Years later, as another missionary spoke to a native tribe about the story of Jesus, he was interrupted by an old woman. "Oh, wait a minute," she said, "that man was here. He visited our village some years ago." Her recollection of Livingston connected her to the story of Jesus.[7] At the end of my earthly journey, I hope somebody will remember me that way. Don't you?

Notes

1. Frederick Buechner, *Peculiar Treasures* (San Francisco: Harper and Row, 1979), pp. 121-23.

2. Evelyn Benet, *New Beginnings* (Old Tappan, N.J.: Fleming H. Revell, 1988), p. 189.

3. Cited in William Richard Ezell, "It's a Wonderful Life," *Preaching* (November/December 1996), p. 47.

4. Ernest E. Mosley, "Don't Assume They Understand," *The Baptist Program* (February 1990): 26.

5. H. Eddie Fox and George E. Morris, *Faith-Sharing* (Nashville: Discipleship Resources, 1993), pp. 79-80.

6. Robert Wuthnow, *God and Mammon in America* (New York: Macmillan, 1994), p. 100.

7. Bruce Larson, *The Communicator's Commentary: Luke* (Waco: Word Books, 1983), p. 238.

Chapter 6

With Some Wannabes

Luke 9:57-62

Somewhere I read about a surefire marketing scheme that missed. A large department store tried marketing a Baby Jesus doll. I guess it was a Christmas promotion. The ads described the doll as being "washable, cuddly, and unbreakable." It was neatly packaged in satin, straw, and plastic, and the package included biblical texts appropriate to Baby Jesus. The idea looked like a moneymaker to department store executives, but they were wrong. It did not sell. In a last-ditch effort to move the unsold dolls, a store manager put them on display under a huge sign:

Jesus Christ
Marked down 50%!
Get him while you can!

That's the sort of bargain the world has been seeking for a long time—as far back as the New Testament itself.

The encounter before us could be called "Jesus and the Wannabes." (I looked up *wannabe* in Webster's. It's not there, but it is one of those slang expressions that has worked its way into common usage.) Here we meet three people who talk about putting their trust in Jesus, who "wannabe" his followers. But Jesus says, "Discipleship is not cheap. There are no markdowns." There is a harsh tone to this text. Something about it does not

feel fair or feel right or feel like Jesus. I suspect that like a lot of
other conversations in the Gospels, this one includes only snip-
pets of the actual encounter that it describes. Luke emphasizes
that Jesus has "set his face to go to Jerusalem" for the final
showdown and the cross (Luke 9:51). So these three conversations are roadside encounters, and I wish we knew more about
the people involved. If we knew all of the circumstances here,
Jesus' words might have a different ring to them—or they might
not.

What does Jesus say here? Look before you leap; count the
cost before you buy; don't "buy a pig in a poke" (to recall my
Alabama roots). This story tells us that faith sharing is not to be
market driven and seeker friendly only. Certainly we need to be
marketwise in reaching out to unchurched Americans, but we
need to be Christ driven as well. What does it mean to be Christ
driven? These brief encounters suggest that it means being clear,
honest, and realistic.

Look at the story. Matthew's account calls the first person a
scribe. Scribes make the rules, write the rules, and keep the rules.
Scribes have watched Jesus break the rules—eating with sinners,
touching lepers, keeping company with poor folks and women
and traitorous tax collectors. So it's pretty amazing that this
scribe says, "I'll follow you anywhere." And Jesus, who has just
been refused lodging in Samaria, says, "I can't give you an
address. Animals and birds have addresses, but I do not."

So this is not a gospel of prosperity. It's not a "name it and
claim it" power message. Jesus' invitation to follow leads to
neither glamour nor security. It's an invitation to the road, to the
unknown, to the not yet. A well-ordered, well-defined person like
this scribe might well find that totally unthinkable. On the other
hand, it might be the spiritual challenge he's been waiting for all
his life! Luke does not tell us how he decides.

The second person hears Jesus' invitation to follow and says,
"OK, provided you leave my values and assumptions alone." The
expression "let me go first and bury my father" does not refer to

an impending funeral. Rather, it refers to a son's most sacred obligation to his father—to see that he has a decent burial and that his affairs are settled. William Barclay recalls that a brilliant young Arab once used similar words in refusing a scholarship to a British university: "Only when I've buried my father."[1] I recently baptized a young Japanese woman who is convinced that her husband (also a believer) will not be baptized until his Buddhist mother dies.

I can imagine this man's feelings. "Who knows where Jesus is headed? Following him might take me away from my traditions, my heritage, and my past. I'm not sure I'm ready for the kind of change that might bring." Thy kingdom come, thy will be done, but not now and not for a while, and certainly not in any way that would upset the way things are "supposed to be."

Jesus talks about making a break with the past: "Some folks will stay entombed in the way it's always been. Let them be—the dead can bury the dead. The status quo will support . . . the status quo. As for you, if you're willing, there is a fresh new way to live. It's God's kingdom. Come, taste, follow, and tell others!" (Luke 9:60) Was this man really looking for a change? Or did he settle for the familiar, comfortable way of his past? Did he pass up the great adventure Jesus was offering? Luke doesn't tell us.

The last person Jesus meets along the roadside wants to follow him, but only after saying good-bye to the folks back home. What's wrong with that? Nothing. But Jesus says, "We're talking about a different way of living here because there's a different goal for living here." I haven't plowed much in my life, but I know enough about it to know that Jesus is on target. You *look ahead* to the end of the row, not back over your shoulder. If you keep looking back or down or to the side, your row will be crooked. The best way to keep it straight is to keep looking ahead.

"Following me," says Jesus to this wannabe disciple, "will not be easy under the best of circumstances, but it will be impossible without your full focus on the goal." In the kingdom of God you travel with your eyes to the front because life in the kingdom is about a personal relationship with God, about community despite barriers, about ministry, about giving more than getting, about loving people enough to shoulder crosses, and about doing the right and the good and the just thing—based on the standards of Christ, not society.

You can't live this life on your own. You can't depend on your background or your culture. You can live this life only by looking ahead to Jesus. So the folks who are "fit for the kingdom," as Jesus puts it here, are not the perfect folks. They're the pilgrim folks, the plowing folks who live toward goodness and by grace. Does this person get it? Luke doesn't say. Jesus moves on. These quick encounters pass into the record, and we are left wondering who followed and who didn't.

Christ's whole life was God's invitation to enter the kingdom, to follow him into discipleship. Everybody is invited; anybody is welcome. Not everybody will choose to follow and grow and be changed. Jesus was faithful in urging people to follow, but the record shows that he did not force the issue. People have to make their own decisions about discipleship.

This short story teaches a couple of lessons about faith sharing. One is, *Speak the truth.* Jesus confronts these three people about discipleship verbally. I often hear people talk about the "witness of a life," as if words were unnecessary. Which is more important: my life or my words? Obviously, both are important. Someone put it this way: which tire matters more on your bicycle—the front or the back? Which wing is more important to an airplane—the right wing or the left? Life and words go together, but here Jesus clearly speaks.

Still some resist. "I don't need to talk about my faith. When you look at my life, you'll see everything you need to know about my faith." That's not true and it's not accurate, not even for Jesus. There are times when Jesus' words explained his life. He goes home with Zacchaeus. He drinks Samaritan water. The actions may come first, but he always talks. In the story before us he speaks first and speaks clearly. I like the way George Sweazey put it in one of his books on evangelism:

> It is not entirely modest to say, "I don't need to talk about Christ; when you look at me, you'll see all of him you need to know." No one lives out an adequate witness to the Christian faith. You cannot, just by being good, reveal that Jesus Christ is the divine savior who died for your sins and now lives as your Lord and ever-present helper. No congregation is so radiant an embodiment of Christ that people can be transformed just by observing it.[2]

Words are important in faith sharing because those unchurched Americans who come within range of our witness are loaded down with assumptions and predispositions, just like these three whom Jesus met on the road. Some of these assumptions are accurate, but, as with the people Jesus encountered, many are not. Some people have heard the prosperity gospel: "You'll be happy and successful and wealthy if you do the right thing." Some have heard of a vengeful God, while others have heard of a permissive God. Some think a Christian must be perfect, and when they meet Christians who clearly are not perfect, they wonder what kind of a phony game they are playing. What about dying? What about sin? What set of beliefs must I bend my mind to? The invitation to Christian discipleship is an invitation to a journey of growth and change. Folks need to know that. Tell them the truth. The people you love and reach out to deserve that.

Many years ago, when Baptist counselor Lofton Hudson spoke about understanding people, he said something that has stayed with me. When some folks tell what Christ means to them, he said, they sound like a television commercial that guarantees success to all who use the product. Overselling is dishonest, and it alienates the customer. Just them *your* story. Life is not a charmed affair for any of us. Being a Christian did not save your marriage or your kids. Being a Christian did not insulate you from disease or disappointment. But Christian faith *is* authentic truth, tested in the fires of our experiences. My life is full, not empty, because I'm a believer. My journey has meaning, not meaninglessness, because I'm a Christian. In an age that knows much of despair, I live with solid hope. I cannot argue anybody into faith, but on the strength of how I've traveled, I can give you reason to take Christ's claims seriously. Most people welcome honesty and clarity. Kirkegaard said of Friedrich Hegel, the early nineteenth-century philosopher, that if you asked him for a street address in Copenhagen, he would hand you a map of Europe! We must do better than that as we share our faith.

I heard about an opera singer who went to a New York post office one day to pick up a package. The singer had neglected to bring any identification, and the clerk adamantly refused to turn over the package. "All right," she said, "I'll show you who I am." She stepped back from the counter and started to sing an aria for which she was well known. A crowd quickly gathered around to listen, and before long the clerk said, "Fine, lady, OK! You can have the package. Just please be quiet!" The time will come to tell the truth regarding who we are and what our lives are about.

The other lesson that Jesus' encounter teaches us, simply put, is to *live the truth.* Jesus would never have had the opportunity to say what he said in these encounters without the impact of his life. These three persons on the roadside were drawn to him by his life, however little or however much they knew about it. Unchurched Americans are looking for the real thing—for people who look something like Jesus; people who live by love instead of selfishness; people who do right, whether or not it makes headlines. They want to know if we're serious. "You worship how often? Invest how much of yourself? Dirty your hands with what needs?" We make the greatest impact when we view all of life as an opportunity of grace and joy and hope. If we live the truth, the opportunity to talk will usually come—after time and prayer and listening.

Tony Campolo is a popular teacher, writer, and speaker. He once made a trip to Honolulu that he has referred to on more than one occasion. Suffering from jet lag, Campolo found himself wide awake and hungry at 3:30 in the morning. He left his hotel to find something to eat and discovered an all-night diner with stools and a counter. The man behind the counter wiped his hands on a grease-stained apron and asked, "What will you have?"

"Just a cup of coffee and a doughnut," replied Campolo. Suddenly a group of eight or nine boisterous women burst in the door and sat down on the stools along the counter, laughing and talking. Realizing they were prostitutes, Campolo started thinking about a way to make his exit as quickly as possible. As he finished his coffee, the woman seated next to him said, "Tomorrow's my birthday; I'll be thirty-nine." From down the counter, another woman said, "Big deal! So what do you want? A cake, a party, somebody singing 'Happy Birthday'?"

"I'm not asking for anything," she said. "I've never had a birthday party in all my life. Why now?" They left soon, and Campolo asked Harry, the man behind the counter, "Do they come here every night?"

"Yes," he replied. "I know them well. That's Agnes who's having the birthday. Why do you ask?"

"Well," said his customer, "what do you say we have a birthday party right here tomorrow night?" Harry smiled and called his wife out from the kitchen to tell her. Campolo told them he'd be back at 2:30 the next morning with a cake and decorations. "No," said Harry. "We'll make the cake."

By the next night the word was out on the street, and at 3:15 a.m. the diner was packed with street people and prostitutes. Campolo had strung up crepe paper and a big sign that read Happy Birthday, Agnes. When she walked in, everyone shouted. She was so surprised her knees buckled, and someone had to help her to a seat. Her eyes started to fill, and when they brought in the cake, Agnes broke into sobs. She said she couldn't blow out the candles, and someone else did it for her. Agnes couldn't take her eyes off the cake. "Before we cut it, can I take it home for a little while? I just live down the street." As the door closed behind Agnes, a deep silence fell over the diner. Campolo broke it by saying, "What do you say we pray for Agnes?" He prayed for her life to change, for God to be good to her, and for her salvation. After he finished, Harry said, "You didn't tell me you were a preacher. What church do you belong to?" Campolo didn't answer right away. After a moment, he said, "I belong to the church that throws birthday parties for prostitutes at 3:30 in the morning." The man sneered, "No, you don't. There's no church like that. If there was, I'd join it."

You just can't beat living the truth and telling the truth! It's the way Jesus, a friend of sinners, shared *his* faith.

Notes

1. William Barclay, *The Gospel of Luke* (Philadelphia: Westminster, 1956), p. 133.

2. George Sweazey, *The Church as Evangelist* (New York: Harper and Row, 1978), p. 34.

CHAPTER 7

With a Seeker

John 1:35-42

The first chapter of John's Gospel is chock-full of faith sharers. There's John the Baptizer. When Jesus walks by, John turns to two persons who have been part of his own renewal movement and says, "He's the one! It's time for the next step. Go!" There's Andrew. Some translations of verse 41 say that "first thing the next morning" he went looking for Simon his brother to bring him to Jesus. Later there's Philip. He's a home-towner with Andrew and Simon Peter. He's the one who goes to his friend Nathanael to say, "The one we have been looking for is here—come and see."

There are times when personal witness occurs spontaneously with people we barely know, but usually witness follows the trail of personal friendships and relationships. That's the way it happens in the story before us.

But the longer we have been Christians, the fewer non-Christians we know. New friendships within the church start replacing old ones. Church activities and commitments become an important part of our schedule. We find ourselves traveling in circles that include unbelievers less and less. That's why some of the most effective faith sharing often happens within the first year or two of a believer's experience in Christ. It's also why we must be very intentional about establishing relationships with unchurched Americans.

As our passage in John indicates, personal witness is telling what we know and sharing what we have experienced. John, Andrew, Philip all say, "Look, here's how I see Jesus. Here's my story." A lot of the time the Bible can be part of that story. There's Bible here, all right, but there's also a need for explanation.

> *Philip found Nathanael and said to him, "We have found him about whom Moses in the law and also the prophets wrote, Jesus son of Joseph from Nazareth." Nathanael said to him, "Can anything good come out of Nazareth?" Philip said to him, "Come and see." (John 1:45-46)*

The Hebrew Bible never mentions Nazareth in connection with the coming Messiah. Philip nevertheless uses Scripture, but he uses personal experience as well. "I found the One, Nathanael," he says, "but you'll have to come and see for yourself." I am making this point because sometimes Scripture is useful in faith sharing and sometimes not. But using Scripture is never automatic or magical. Many years ago a church newsletter came across my desk that included articles that told about an unusual use of Scripture. One of the ministers in the church that published the newsletter had gone to the West Coast to launch a fifteen-month "Bible memory crusade" in the churches there. The course was called "The Treasure Path to Soul Winning," and the optimistic minister wrote, "From past experience I have learned that every twenty verses memorized results in one soul saved per year. If all the pastors are faithful to reach their desired goals, I expect to see a harvest of 13,038 souls in heaven as a result of this program." Of course, every pastor who reaches his goal also gets a free trip to the Holy Land![1] I have no comment, except to say that I have not experienced such a result from using Scripture!

What we can do, I think, is use a "plan of salvation" from Scripture—maybe three or four sections or only one. I have sometimes used John 3:16 as my "plan of salvation." That text is useful in telling the whole story of sin and salvation. You could make similar use of other single verses in the New Testament (for example, Romans 3:23; 10:9; Acts 16:31). But whatever you memorize or quote, *make it yours.* Lead with your own faith experience and filter the Scripture through that. Generalities don't help much; specifics do. "Where is God?" the little girl asked. "God is everywhere," said her mother. Troubled, the child responded, "But I don't want God to be everywhere. I want God to be somewhere!" How do issues like sin, guilt, God's love, and belief look from behind your eyes and inside your skin? How do Bible words make sense in your experience? What connection do you make between biblical terms and daily life? How has being a believer made a difference in your own life journey thus far?

Sam Shoemaker said that the test of our personal conversion is whether we have "enough Christianity to get it over to other people." The test is really this, he wrote: "Can I get across to other people what I believe about Jesus Christ? If not, what good am I to them, and what real good am I to Him?"[2] Faith sharing follows the trail of personal relationships, and it speaks the language of personal story.

Andrew is a seeker. Actually, there are two of them in this story, but there is no way of knowing who the other person is—older or younger, female or male. John, the writer of the Gospel, may be the other individual. John is designated the "beloved disciple" three times in the Gospel that bears his name. Perhaps that explains some of the details in the story. It's as if John is saying, "I remember a spring afternoon. I remember that it was about four o'clock, when I turned the most significant corner of my life. Here's what happened!"

I can't prove it, but I think this story happened before that time described in Matthew's and Mark's accounts when Jesus passes by the Sea of Galilee and calls out to Peter, James, John, and Andrew. This earlier encounter occurs a few miles to the south and near the river where John the Baptizer is preaching. My hunch is that Andrew, his unnamed friend, and Simon, his brother, all go back to the fishing fleet to talk about this meeting with Jesus—what they saw and heard and felt.

In the Gospels it is clear that there are some folks whom Jesus approaches first. He takes the initiative. There is Zacchaeus, the Samaritan woman, Matthew the tax collector, several people who are sick. There are others, however, who seek him out. Why they seek him varies. His family probably came to take him home and save him from embarrassing himself. Nicodemus is a religious leader who likely came to check out his orthodoxy. The woman in the crowd reached out to touch his robe with a desperate hope for her own healing. Andrew and his unnamed friend come to Jesus for none of those reasons. Their hearts are hungry, and they are ready for some answers.

The term *seeker* is often used to designate the hungry hearted in our own time. Contemporary pundits refer to ours as a "postmodern" age. This does not mean that large numbers of our contemporaries have rejected things like reason, logic, or technology. What they do seem to be rejecting is the assumption that such things alone can be the center of a human life. Seekers in search of a center have sprung up by the thousands in the fertile soil of postmodernism. There was a time around the turn of the century when most everybody believed that the emergent "modern era" would solve most of our problems and offer us the most purposeful lives imaginable. Harry Emerson Fosdick recalls the words spoken by a distinguished American professor in 1912: "Today we have no fear of war, famine, pestilence, or failing resources. The advance of knowledge has safeguarded men from all of those evils."[3] Despite handing us more technological resources than ever before, modernism has not delivered on all of its promises. Consumption, speed, technology, and affluence are characteristics of our century, yet they cannot guarantee us lives of fulfillment. In their monumental work, *Habits of the Heart*, Robert Bellah and his colleagues concluded that modernism's "blessings" are mixed at best:

There is a widespread feeling that the promise of the Modern Era is slipping away from us. A movement of enlightenment and liberation that was to have freed us from superstition and tyranny has led in the Twentieth Century to a world in which ideological fanaticism and political oppression have reached extremes unknown in previous history. Science, which was to have unlocked the bounties of nature, has given us the power to destroy all life on Earth. Progress, modernity's master idea, seems less compelling when it appears that it may be progress into the abyss.[4]

This gnawing dissatisfaction with the answers that modernity provided has bred a flock of seekers in American society. They crave answers for the inner life—solutions of the spirit. "Despair," said a pastoral colleague recently, "is not the answer, it's the question." I believe that Andrew's pursuit of his dissatisfaction and yearning led him to Jesus.

Let's study what Jesus does to share his faith with these seekers—Andrew and his unnamed friend. *Jesus starts where they are.* "What are you looking for?" he asks them. They simply want an address. "Where are you staying?" But Jesus starts there. Seekers show up these days in the places where we worship, where we do Bible study, where we minister to the homeless, or in other places around our churches. Like Andrew, they have lived themselves into Jesus' question: "What are you looking for?" Many of them feel drawn to the church (or back to the church) because they have discovered life issues that demand more than a biological or technological explanation. There are moments when we know that we are more than protoplasm and brain functioning. These moments lead us to a spiritual search. It's a hunger for the transcendent—something beyond cold logic and rationality.

This hunger can hit you at the strangest times: watching a movie, soaring at a symphony, seeing a painting or a piece of sculpture. It may be a line in a book or a play or a song. In our secularized society, which may not put much stock in religion, art and music and media allow us to speak of, to listen for, and to be surprised by holy things. However we encounter them, there are great, deep questions that turn unchurched Americans into seekers. These questions are often heard and experienced as a vague restlessness or an unfocused cloud of longing. They ask about our origins, our destiny, our purpose, our dying, and eternity. There's a part of Leonard Bernstein's *Mass* that says:

What I need I don't have,
What I have I don't own,
What I own I don't want,
What I want, Lord, I don't know.

Andrew is drawn to Jesus by the hoped-for, the not-yet of his life. Like the singer in the *Mass,* he might have trouble putting it into words, but it's there—the longing, the thirst, the groping after God.

Even before we know how to name it, our need for God is there. It's the aching void of every life. It is a feeling that is miserable or empty or frustrated or hopeless or angry or guilty. So we cry out, "Where is a grace that will meet me where I hurt?" Our culture offers its answers to this question with, Take a pill, have a drink, join a gym, change jobs, get a divorce, move away, try harder. As if the void that aches *inside* us is about surroundings or physical strength or heredity or economics. But it's not about any of that. It's about the Great Mystery and my life and about some kind of connection between the two that will give me some lasting direction. I think that's how Andrew got to Jesus.

And it wasn't as if he didn't have other options. If he had wanted conventional religion, he could have stayed with traditional Judaism. If he had wanted a more demanding lifestyle, he could have worked to become a Pharisee. If he had wanted political leverage, he could have joined the Zealots or some other vigilante group. If he had wanted dissenting and unconventional religion, he could have stayed with John the Baptizer. But when John sees Jesus and says, "Look, God's Lamb," Andrew follows his restlessness toward Jesus.

And Jesus starts with Andrew's longing. He asks the pivotal

question, "What are you looking for?" Does Andrew really understand the sort of hunger that has led him to this moment? I doubt that it's fully focused for him any more than for our contemporary seekers. Sometimes it comes in a hurt and a need for healing. Sometimes it's loneliness and a need for community. Sometimes it's guilt and a need for forgiveness. Sometimes it's the nagging questions about the deep issues of life. And sometimes people become seekers just because a touch of transcendence has fallen over their souls somehow, and they are curious to know more. One of the things that we seasoned, church-involved, busy Christians often forget is how the need for beginning faith is felt and perceived, and how badly people want to find it.

So seekers often show up where we are staying or, at least, at the church house where we spend some of our time. An interesting recent trend is the development of seeker-sensitive or seeker-friendly worship services. The assumption is that many seekers have little or no familiarity with traditional Christian liturgy, and church dropouts will find it more comfortable to return to a contemporary style of worship. Conclusion? The sights and sounds of worship are more palatable to seekers when they are compatible with life in the "real world." Worship music has the sound of soft rock, usually accompanied by various instruments and rhythmic clapping. Dress is casual. Preaching is conversational and deals almost exclusively with personal lifestyle issues, often supplemented by dramatic or video vignettes. The offering, if it is taken at all, is incidental. As befits a generation reared on television sitcoms and sound bites, everything in the service moves at a fast, smooth, carefully choreographed pace.

Early statistical results from such seeker-friendly worship styles are certainly impressive. Long-range, however, it remains to be seen whether this approach to worship as evangelism will continue to nourish the souls it has touched and won. Here's what I'm driving at. Baby boomers and busters tend to be consumer conscious. They have grown up not only in a world of technology with its quick fixes but also in a world that has known scarcity and shortage as well. Consequently, whatever feels *right*, offers quick answers, and lifts their spirits will appeal to these church shoppers. Denominational labels become irrelevant; the local congregation is everything. These days, historian Leon McBeth says, "people no longer choose church by brand name. Members and ministers are increasingly interchangeable."[5] One result in such a scenario is that some market-driven, seeker-friendly churches put minimal emphasis on theological formation and reflection. In a *Newsweek* article historian Martin Marty cautions, "To give the whole store away to match what this year's market says the unchurched want is to have the people who know least about faith determine most about its expression."[6] In the same magazine essayist Kenneth Woodward concludes, "The mainline denominations may be dying because they lost their theological integrity. The only thing worse, perhaps, would be the rise of a new Protestant establishment that succeeds because *it never had any.*"[7]

So one of the concerns in such a scenario is that market-driven, seeker-friendly churches will be tempted to put minimal emphasis on theological reflection and character formation. Marva J. Dawn warns that worship practices that foster good feelings and instant gratification could be self-defeating: "A focus on self and feelings limits the nurturing of a godly and outreaching character." Thus, the same methods that draw crowds "might also prevent the development of habits of reflection and learning."[8] The gospel of Jesus Christ, she concludes, "is indeed attractive to the unsaved, but we cannot sow it in shallowness if we want to reap deep discipleship."[9]

One of the strongest voices of dissent belongs to Eugene H. Peterson. Though his words are addressed primarily to pastors, all believers need to hear and weigh them. Peterson believes that many Americans view God as "a product that will help them to live well, or to live better."[10] Thus pastors are strongly tempted to "start making deals, packaging the God-product so that people will be attracted to it, and then presenting it in ways that will beat out the competition."[11] The danger in such an atmosphere, Peterson concludes, is that pastors growing up in it will be largely uncritical of it, never realizing that "it is the good old free-enterprise system that works so well for everyone except the poor and a few minorities."[12]

Russell Chandler worked for several years on the *Los Angeles Times* staff as a religion specialist. I met him one morning in 1993 while attending a conference in Florida; we were seated next to each other. We introduced ourselves at the end of the session and exchanged information about our work. In the course of our conversation, I told him about my book, *The Struggle To Believe,* which targeted believers who had dropped out of church and their need to rethink faith concepts.[13] He went on to tell me that his 1992 release, *Racing Toward 2001,* examined similar issues. On the strength of that brief encounter, I bought a copy of Chandler's book. It is a cogent and helpful analysis of American religious life at the end of the twentieth century. He applauds the effective outreach of evangelical churches that are savvy in marketing and communication skills. He warns that such consumer-oriented churches are tempted to turn Christian faith into a matter of individual acquisitiveness. He recalls Tom Sine's assertion that "the Evangelical Church is being co-opted slowly by the American dream—do it all and have it all—with a little Jesus overlay."[14] The shallowness of such an approach was borne out by a 1990 Roper survey that tested the actions of born-again Christians before and after their conversion experiences. The conclusion was jarring: conversion apparently made very little behavioral difference. This particular study found that the use of illegal drugs, driving while intoxicated, and marital infidelity actually *increased* after the born-again experience![15] When it comes to life-changing faith, a quick fix never really does!

Whether your church offers a more contemporary worship option or not, all of us should be on the lookout for ways to welcome the stranger and the seeker among us. It's not easy.

Examining "the way we've always done it" with a view toward helping the seeker's quest can be difficult. I have worshiped in churches where I needed three hands just to keep up with the liturgical paraphernalia. I have been in settings where worship leaders seemed intent on stirring my emotions and unplugging my brain. Like most people, I have visited far too many churches where nobody smiled, spoke, or seemed to care who I was or why I was there. I recently found a tongue-in-cheek list of ways to assure that seekers do not feel welcome in worship. This list cuts across all liturgical lines.

1. Stare and glare to make newcomers feel uneasy and unwelcome.
2. Have members gather in tight groups and ignore visitors.
3. Always crowd into the back pews so that visitors must be ushered up front where they can be stared at.
4. Welcome only people who are of your own race and are at or above your own income level.
5. Remember that only official greeters should welcome visitors because that's their job.
6. Make sure that only men serve as worship leaders so that women, youth, and children feel left out.
7. Never help newcomers who may become confused about the order of worship; it's good for them to flounder.

By following this list, you will certainly avoid any of the excesses of seeker-friendly worship!

Is the Christian faith capable of addressing the yearning and restlessness of seekers such as Andrew? My answer is a ringing yes! We can accomplish this by emulating Jesus' next action in this encounter, namely, *he makes himself available.* "Come and see," he says. And these two people spend the next few hours in his company. Jesus starts where Andrew and his friend are, but he leads them toward this clarifying, sorting-out time.

The late afternoon visit in Jesus' quarters might have started with that first question. "Andrew, what are you really looking for? Do you know? Will it work? What have you tried?" Andrew may have come hoping for a political revolution or a social reformation or a religious revival or simply feeling curious. I imagine they talked about all of that. The crucial thing is that Jesus makes himself available to these seekers. He lets them inside his own life and feelings and schedule. "Come and see," the text says, "come closer and see that I'm for real."

Seekers and unchurched people want to know that. "Is this faith stuff real? Can you tell me about it in a plain way?" Even more important, they are wondering, "Are *you* for real? Does your humanity look and feel like my humanity?"

Henri Nouwen tells a story about going to the same restaurant for lunch every day. It was a pretty dull place, but there was a beautiful red rose in a small vase in the middle of the table where Nouwen always sat. He enjoyed the rose and even came to talk to it each day. "But then," Nouwen says, "I became suspicious. Because while my mood was changing during the week from happy to sad, from disappointed to angry, from energetic to apathetic, my rose was always the same." He got suspicious and finally touched the rose, to find that it was plastic. He never went back there to eat.[16]

Believers and churches cannot answer every question or meet every need, but we can be real. We can be human and we can be available to people who are seeking after faith. The necessary spiritual sorting out will get done on the basis of trust and friendship.

In personal relationships over the years, I have been able to ask questions like these: How are you dealing with this struggle? Have you ever thought about becoming a Christian? What is your understanding of God? I get all kinds of responses, such as, What do you mean? I grew up Baptist or Catholic or something else. I don't know much about God or religion—I've never thought about it. I believe in God—I'm an American, after all. I recall a conversation with a man who told me that he encouraged his children to develop their faith based on belief in God and in the Constitution of the United States. Every such reply opens up the possibility of faith sharing, provided we are willing to follow Jesus' lead and take the time to be available.

Where the sun shines in the street
There are very many feet
Seeking God.
All unaware that their hastening is a prayer.
Perhaps those folks would deem it odd
Who think they are on business bent,
If someone went
And told them "You are seeking God."[17]

To tell unchurched Americans that, we must be intentional and available. Jesus was. One final important word. When, like Andrew, seekers decide to become believers, we need to travel with them further down the road. Converts don't become disciples quickly or easily, and our availability must not come to a screeching halt after they have walked back up the aisle or out of the baptistry.

A guide had been leading a hunting party deeper and deeper into the woods. Finally he threw up his hands and declared, "We're lost." One of the people in the hunting party screamed, "Lost! You told me you were the best guide in the whole country!"

"I am," the guide said, "but we're in Canada now." When we share our faith, our availability and guidance do not turn back at any border. Following Jesus is the great and exciting journey of a lifetime, and we need to stick together!

Notes

1. J. O. Grooms, "Soul Winning," *Word of Life* [newsletter of the Thomas Road Baptist Church, Lynchburg, Virginia], 1 September 1971, p. 3.

2. Sam Shoemaker, *How to Become a Christian* (New York: Harper and Brothers, 1953), p. 74.

3. Harry Emerson Fosdick, *A Great Time to Be Alive* (New York: Harper and Brothers, 1944), p. 204.

4. Robert Bellah et al., *Habits of the Heart* (New York: Harper and Row, 1985), p. 277.

5. Marv Knox, "Social Trends Shaping Church of Tomorrow, McBeth Says," Associated Baptist press release, 12 July 1996.

6. Martin Marty, cited in Kenneth L. Woodward, "Dead End for the Mainline?" *Newsweek,* 9 August 1993, p. 48.

7. Ibid. Italics are mine.

8. *Reaching Out without Dumbing Down* (Grand Rapids: William B. Eerdmans, 1995), p. 111.

9. Ibid., p. 45.

10. Eugene H. Peterson, *Under the Predictable Plant* (Grand Rapids: Eerdmans, 1992), p. 35.

11. Ibid., p. 36.

12. Ibid.

13. William L. Turner, *The Struggle to Believe* (Macon, Ga.: Smyth and Helwys, 1993).

14. Tom Sine, cited in R*acing Toward 2001* by Russell Chandler (Grand Rapids and San Francisco: Zondervan and Harper, 1992), p. 165.

15. Ibid., pp. 165-66.

16. Henri Nouwen, *Creative Ministry* (New York: Image Books, 1971), p. 105.

17. Mary Carolyn Davies, in *Sermons Preached in a University Church,* by George Buttrick (New York: Abingdon, 1959), pp. 158-59.

Chapter 8

With a Cynical Bureaucrat

John 18:28—19:2

Three expectant fathers were sitting in a maternity waiting room. The nurse came out and said to one man, "Sir, you're the father of twins. Congratulations!" He said, "That's amazing because I'm a member of the Minnesota Twins baseball team." A little later she came out and said to a second man, "Sir, congratulations! You are the father of triplets." He said, "Amazing! I work for the 3M Company." At that point the third man started running for the door. "I'm getting out of here," he said. "I work for Seven-Up!" Sometimes you can predict what's going to happen, and it can be scary!

Pontius Pilate, governor of Judea in the first century, could not have predicted the outcome of his encounter with one Jesus, a rabbi from Nazareth. Herod Antipas, son of Herod the Great, sits on the Jewish throne by permission of Rome. Herod plays with this prisoner and then sends him to Pilate (only a person who receives thumbs-down from Rome can be executed). Neither Pilate nor Herod could have seen the outcome of it all. Imagine the talk over dinner years later as they recall, "We had our moments, didn't we? Pretenders to the throne, claims of kingship, stormy politics, would-be messiahs. Then there was *that one* from Nazareth in Galilee. What was his name, the teacher?" They could not have dreamed that the world would remember them precisely and only because of that one prisoner. Long after Pilate's Caesar is forgotten, this teacher's truth remains more powerful than any ruler ever was.

Pilate is one of the few secularists we meet in the New Testament. Most persons in the Jesus story and the early church story are associated with some kind of religious tradition. Pilate is Roman. Maybe he's religious, maybe he's not. Rome had plenty of gods and goddesses, but they didn't matter much to most folks, particularly after the Caesars declared themselves to be gods and sons of the gods. People saw through that rather easily—religion pressed into the service of politics. Whenever religion is reduced to blessing the status quo, it becomes phony. So people were left spiritually empty.

Kenneth Scott Latourette, arguably the greatest church historian of the twentieth century, tells how the early church, despite the obstacles it faced, was able to expand in the Roman Empire. Early Christians recognized several dominant needs that people had, and they were able to relate the message of the Gospel to those needs. One problem was loneliness. As the empire expanded, many Romans became separated from home and clan. They were drawn to the love and fellowship of the early church. There was an ongoing quest for truth that expressed itself in a variety of religions, philosophies, and cults. The first-century Roman world also had a need for God. Skeptical of emperor worship, people worshiped unknown gods in a search for meaning. They were also looking for a higher moral standard in their decadent society. The early Christian message that we can be empowered by Christ to live a new life was attractive. There was also a widespread desire for immortality. The religions of the day did not offer much hope for life after death. Latourette contends that Christianity prevailed in the Roman world because it engaged these deepest personal needs more clearly and explicitly than all competing religions.[1]

But Pilate, a man of his time, comes across as a cynical bureaucrat. He is a middle manager—the Roman administrator of a province that is anything but a plum assignment. He does what Rome wants to have done, and that means establishing peace and unity. Rome prided itself in the administration of "impartial justice." But that was not achieved in the case of Jesus. Maybe it was because Pilate did not care (nonbiblical evidence reveals his clear disdain for these Judeans he ruled). Maybe injustice prevailed because Pilate lacked courage. Three times in the trial stories of the Gospels, Pilate says, "This man is not a criminal." Yet because Herod had great influence with Caesar (and Herod was inclined to execute this prisoner), Pilate caved in and did the expedient thing. Fair-minded people, acting out of expedience, do raise crosses and drive nails.

Pilate was not open to change, even to serve justice. He was given to maintaining and time serving and pleasing the powers that be. He did that in Judea for nine, ten years, and then finished his career elsewhere. Yet Judea was filled with wild fanaticisms and strange fundamentalisms. This Passover season seemed to be a ticking time bomb. Pilate usually stayed in Caesarea, but during this hectic Passover he went to Jerusalem under escort of the Roman army; his headquarters were in a place called the Praetorium, near the temple. Here he met Jesus.

That Pilate was a Roman bureaucrat is a fact of history. That he was secular and cynical is my own personal assessment. I read him as someone who had been around the block—someone who had lived long enough and had seen and done enough to be jaded about life. Albert Einstein was fond of saying that the best thing we can experience is a sense of the mysterious. The impenetrable does exist, even if we can speak of it in story and symbol only. I have observed that cynicism usually comes into life when wonder goes out of it. Cynicism rules out surprises. A cynic believes that life means nothing (so why bother?) or that life means something (but we'll never find it or know it or do it). You can meet the cynic in the courtroom, in the classroom, in the boardroom, on the job, and elsewhere—the sneering and sighing ones who find no meaning to life.

Look how Jesus shares his faith with this person in this situation. First, *he's real*. He doesn't argue with Pilate, and he doesn't compromise his own values. What he says to him is this: "I'm not about a political or military kingdom. I'm not leading my disciples toward an insurrection. I've come to bear witness to a life-changing truth about God and about us and about the deeper meaning of life." If you want to know what Jesus is about, look at his life, watch his behavior, look at his moral choices, and observe how he treats people. When he stands before Rome's governor, his life hanging in the balance, he will not be less than what he has been all along.

Unchurched Americans want to know if you and I are real, especially when the chips are down: when it's not easy or popular, when it costs something, when it would be expedient to look the other way, and when conventional wisdom marches to the beat of a cultural or social or economic drummer. The best way to begin sharing your faith with a cynic is to do what Jesus does here—*be real*. Let your own life and lifestyle be the first defense of faith. Nonbelievers won't buy all of the convictions on which you base your life. However, what may be striking and even appealing to them is whether your strongly professed convictions actually shape your behavior and your attitudes, *especially toward them*. In his book *Renewing America's Soul*, Howard E. Butt challenges us to be the kind of people "whose personality patterns are so convincing to skeptics that our witnessing and our evangelism is not hard-sell but merely *explanatory*. We are to live persuasively. Then we are to stay available, modestly, to answer the cynic's questions."[2]

Jesus is also aware: "Then Pilate entered the headquarters again, summoned Jesus, and asked him, 'Are you the King of the Jews?' Jesus answered, 'Do you ask this on your own, or did others tell you about me?'" (John 18:33-34). There are false accusers aplenty in this situation. Jesus knows that. Is Pilate listening to them, or is he going to judge for himself? Jesus knows that his life and his message can be garbled by misinformation and misunderstanding, a lot of it derived from secondhand sources and hearsay.

That much hasn't changed. Some cynical people got that way because of religious misinformation and misunderstandings. When they approached the fires of religion, their fingers were burned in one way or another. They bought into promises about religion that turned out to be nothing but more unmet expectations. So they dropped out, turned off by institutional religion. But they're still (to recall novelist Louise Erdrich's phrase) "seeking somewhere to land their lives."[3] Research shows that a high percentage of church dropouts find religion's claims so weak in comparison to the attractions of the cultural environment that the church simply "slipped off their radar screens. It ceased to be important to them."[4]

In the 1960s the spiritual quest was transformed into support for a cause, such as civil rights, peace, women's equality, ecology. In the 1970s the spiritual turned humanistic—me and my potential. In the 1980s secularism became the spiritual focus, as expressed in popular mottoes: I can make it on my own and Whoever dies with the most toys wins. As the century draws to its close, the spiritual quest goes into the search for jobs or power or new causes. These days the characteristic term seems to be *relativism*—no absolute standards, just whatever works for you. People keep hoping for God to "happen" in their lives in some way. Yet their experience with organized religion (as well as with the many secular and substitute gods) makes them cynical that God ever will.

Thus we are in need of the awareness that Jesus demonstrated. "Pilate, what have you heard about me and how did you hear it? What do you believe and why?" I remember an incident from the ministry of Harry Emerson Fosdick. A young man came to see the well-known pastor to discuss his doubts about religion. "I find," he said, "that I can no longer believe in the existence of God." Wisely, Fosdick responded, "Tell me about that God in which you can no longer believe." As they talked, a sensitive pastor helped a young man discard a lot of unnecessary emotional and intellectual baggage about faith. Sometimes, as with Jesus and Pilate, that's a good starting point for faith sharing. "What do you know? What have you heard? Where did it come from?"

Also—and this is very instructive—*Jesus is silent*. In verse 37 Jesus says, "If you're looking for some fresh truth, listen to me." Pilate won't believe that—not now, not yet, perhaps not ever. "What is truth?" is his cynical rejoinder. Rome's man knows the truth about power: whoever has the biggest army runs the world. He knows the truth about expediency: to get along you go along. He can't imagine anything beyond what he already knows and sees. "What is truth?" he asks, probably meaning, "There are no surprises, right?" And Jesus *does not answer*. Not then, not there, not until, say, Easter morning.

Sometimes cynics need silence and time and the assurance that we respect their autonomy. I really like the straightforward assertion made by British apologist Donald Soper. "I can't argue you to a belief in Jesus Christ; what I have tried to do is to offer you reasonable grounds for taking him seriously. The next step is with you."[5] Meanwhile, cynics need us to do what Jesus does here—lead with the witness of our lives. Our Lord does precisely that, his cross and the empty tomb underscoring his lifelong integrity.

Did any of this matter to Pilate? Did his encounter with Jesus change his life? There's no record that it did. But in the time that he spent with Jesus, Pilate had the truth at close range and the chance to choose. You and I can help make that happen for unchurched Americans, even the cynical ones.

Recalling Kenneth Scott Latourette's catalogue of the needs that unchurched people had in the first century (p.74), I'm struck by its similarity to Kennon Callahan's analysis. As consultant to a variety of congregations, Callahan probably knows as much about church strategy as anybody in our time. He writes that today's people are searching for:

1. Individuality: some sense of personal worth
2. Community: a network and some roots
3. Meaning: some reason to be alive and to keep going
4. Hope: the ability to live beyond despair[6]

Clearly the world has not changed much in two thousand years. Like Pilate of old, a lot of unchurched Americans have given up on having those life needs fulfilled in any lasting way. But we have good news for these folks! Living out of truth and grace ourselves, we may in time earn the opportunity to break the silence with our words. Missionary Nomie Deranie recommends a strategy. "Just love them," she says, "until they ask us why."

A young woman I know is battling a painful and debilitating disease. She had recently been befriended by a woman who is an active church member. They shopped and lunched together, kept in touch by phone, and the friendship deepened. Finally the church member asked, "Why not come to church with me?" The young woman's response was, "I can't, not right now. I'm going through so much. Besides, I'm not even sure there is a God." Since that conversation she has not heard from her friend, the church member. "I guess she was just out to *get* me," she decided. Clearly, loving people means more than "getting" them—and unchurched people are quick to spot the difference!

Every now and then someone who is cynical and hardened by life gets surprised by the truth of God's grace. I read about one such person in an Alabama newspaper. Her story was on the front page—not the religion section, mind you, but the front page. Her name is Martha Hawkins, and she grew up in the deep South as an African American. When she was still a teenager, she became an unwed mother. Later she was married and bore three sons. The marriage ended after eight years, leaving her with four young children. The family lived in a government housing project where drugs and violence were an everyday, every-night fact of life. She struggled to keep her family together—to provide for her children and to make her way in the world. She did this with the help of government welfare, part-time work, and every other resource she could find. But she felt overwhelmed and finally crashed. The boys came home from school one afternoon to find her nearly dead from an overdose of pills.

She was taken to the hospital where her life was saved. About the time she got into therapy, she noticed a Bible on the night-stand. She picked it up one afternoon and started to read. She had tried to read the Bible before, but it never meant much. There had not been enough time to read; her problems had been all-consuming. This time, however, she couldn't put it down. She read all day and into the night. Her therapy continued, along with her Bible reading. What impressed her the most about what she read in the Bible was its consistent theme: God loves me. I am not alone. I can do all things through Christ who strengthens me. That awareness, says Martha Hawkins, began to change her life.

Today in Montgomery, Alabama, Martha's Vineyard is recognized as one of the best eateries in the city. Recalling the feasts she had watched her mother prepare with fresh vegetables, Martha realized that she had a very marketable skill. She began by fixing up an old two-story house, shopping yard sales for used dishes and silverware, and sewing her own napkins and curtains. When she finally obtained a small loan, her dream began to take shape. The restaurant has become a meeting place for politicians, business leaders, and celebrities. Martha left the projects—and welfare—long ago. Her four children are grown up now and doing well. Her conclusions about life are striking. "I have more problems than I ever had, a lot more than when I tried to kill myself," she says. "But I'm not the problem anymore. I feel the Lord has been with me, has been my close friend." Today the customers at Martha's Vineyard eat beneath a simple wall sign. It reads, Taste and see that the Lord is good.[7]

Cynicism, disillusionment, and hopelessness—fertile ground for the Gospel of Jesus Christ! Like Jesus ministering to Pilate, we can be the bearers of a true and fresh alternative.

Notes

1. Kenneth Scott Latourette, cited in H. Eddie Fox and George E. Morris, *Faith-Sharing* (Nashville: Discipleship Resources, 1993), p. 54.

2. Howard E. Butt, *Renewing America's Soul* (Grand Rapids: Fleming H. Revell, 1996), p. 59.

3. Louise Erdrich, cited in Dennis Farney, "Novelist Updike Sees a Nation Frustrated by Its Own Dreams," *The Wall Street Journal,* 16 September 1992, p. 1.

4. Loren B. Mead, *Transforming Congregations for the Future* (New York: Alban Institute, 1994), pp. 15-17.

5. Donald Soper, cited in George G. Hunter III, *How to Reach Secular People* (Nashville: Abingdon, 1992), p. 132.

6. Kennon Callahan, *Twelve Keys to an Effective Church* (San Francisco: Harper and Row, 1983), p. 35.

7. Frank Sikora, "Dream Wins Over Welfare," *The Birmingham News,* April 4, 1995, p. 1A.

CHAPTER 9

Sharing
Our Faith—*with Jesus?*

Matthew 25:31-46

In this last chapter we turn to a story that Jesus tells during his last week in Jerusalem. He talks about what lies ahead for Jerusalem, and then he moves to a series of stories about accountability and judgment. Matthew is the only Gospel that includes this particular story, but there is a first cousin to it in Luke 10—the story of the good Samaritan. The story says that our relationship with Christ is reflected in our relationships with people—especially those in need. It is reflected in how we treat the hungry, the thirsty, the stranger, the naked or destitute, the sick, and the prisoner. We can help people for selfish or for humanitarian reasons. In this passage Jesus is calling for something more. The terms *Son of Man, King,* and *Lord* all refer to himself. He is calling for a way of living that grows directly out of a relationship with him. Those who "pass the test" here are not calculating how to be good, how to please God, or how to gain notoriety. They are intentional about living out of their faith center.

Once a young deacon came to my office for a chat. "Bill," he said, "this is probably the only church in town I can belong to. I want you to know that. Since you're the new pastor, it's my intention—and my family's—to support you fully. But I also want you to know that my goal for our church is to minister to people in this community. Otherwise, it's all a waste of time." I followed that man's life over the years. He takes Jesus seriously by living out his faith in daily ministry to others.

Whatever literal details go with "eternal fire" and "everlasting punishment" in this text, they are (at the very least) the exact opposite of "eternal life." We are given enormous freedom in regard to the choices of life, including the spiritual ones. To be free enough to trust and love God, we must also be free to reject God.

This parable is the only Scripture in which Jesus tells us what he looks like. He looks like the face of human need. "As you did it to one of these, you did it to me." This means that the final sighting of the risen Christ was not in the garden, on the road to Emmaus, in the upper room, or even out on the hillside from which he ascended. Christ sightings are a part of everyday, here-and-now life. You can see him almost anytime—at the clothing center, the food pantry, the medical center, the county jail, the homeless shelter. It's not a literal reincarnation of Christ that we see in hurting people, of course, but Jesus' parable says that wherever else he may show up in this world, the face of the risen Christ will always be a human face, lined with need. It's how we see that face and respond to it that matters most to Christ. That's what this story tells us.

Among those who bear the face of the risen Christ is "the stranger." Granted, the most obvious meaning of the term is those who are homeless. They are travelers who need a place to rest; they are poor and have no permanent place to stay. Some circumstance has created their need for our welcoming hospitality. But the stranger is also the outsider, the uprooted one, the person not included in the family. That person may be poor, hungry, thirsty, sick, destitute, or unkempt. On the other hand, the stranger may wear a suit and tie, an expensive dress, or fashionable sweats and Reeboks. "Strangers to the family of Christ" is another term for the unchurched Americans I have been writing about. They are spiritually homeless and rootless, in search of a center for their lives. The most recent sighting of the risen Christ by any one of us could be in their faces, if we take the time to look at them.

Let us summarize our discussion in the first eight chapters of this book. *First,* we are living in a first-century culture that is urban, secular, pluralistic, and mostly unchurched. The "Christian consensus" of former days is gone, even in the cities of the Bible Belt. Believers live and work on a mission field of enormous possibility, since unchurched Americans now number in the millions. They are young, old, single, and married. A lot of them are not interested in matters of faith—yet! But there are seekers among these strangers:

1. The uprooted and the lonely who are looking for community.

2. The ex-belongers, many of whom just walked away from organized religion. Some are now ready to return to spiritual roots.

3. The never-dids. They did not drop out. They were never in the church, and now they are reevaluating "success." It's not that modernism and materialism and money are "out," it's just that they are not enough. Who knows? Maybe there is a spiritual dimension to living life successfully after all.

Second, there are obstacles. Paul told the Corinthians that he was going to stay in Ephesus a while because there was an open door for faith sharing there, as well as many obstacles (1 Corinthians 16:9). Paul's New Testament situation is ours as well. Consider some of these hindrances.

1. A lot of unchurched Americans dropped out or turned away from the church. Organized religion for them has been confusing at best or damaging at worst. I recently overheard a woman describe how a Baptist worship service had scared her as a child, so she never went back. Sometimes a history of negative personal experiences blocks the way for people.

2. Language can be an obstacle. Much of the language that

speaks to us "insiders" at church is either confusing or alienating to unchurched Americans. We need to do what we have seen Jesus do in all of these stories: listen to the person, listen to the moment, speak plainly. Somewhere I read about a little girl who was instructed by her teacher to construct a sentence using the word *I*. She thought for a moment and then began. "I is," "No, no," interrupted the teacher. "Not 'I is.' Always say 'I am.'"

"OK," she replied. "I am the ninth letter of the alphabet." Like that teacher, we need to learn to listen carefully and speak accordingly.

3. Our relationships can be obstacles too. We church members interact with too many Christians and too few unbelievers. That won't change unless we want it to change and act to change it. Until we do, the stranger will remain invisible and unknown as well as unwelcomed.

Third, as faith sharers we can be Jesus followers. This is the core of everything I have tried to say in this book. Jesus shared his understanding of God with many of the people he met. Sometimes he initiated the relationship, as with the woman at the well and with Zacchaeus in Jericho. Sometimes he responded to what others brought to the encounter: Nicodemus, with his check on Jesus' orthodoxy; Andrew, who just wanted to hear more; a woman bolting out of the crowd, who wanted to touch his garment; and Pilate, who really did not want to be bothered but was there with Jesus. On occasion we have seen Jesus leading with his humanity: "Give me a drink of water" and "I need to stay at your house." Jesus shares his faith in all kinds of settings: the roadside, a dinner table, overnight, a single encounter, a longer relationship. Clearly, Jesus is a person who takes his faith-sharing mission seriously.

He also takes prayer seriously. Long before he listened to the moment and the person, long before he spoke plainly and with impact, Jesus prayed. Scattered throughout the Gospels are times of withdrawal, reflection, and silence. There is no way to know what transpired during those hours and nights of prayer, but they must have included petitions for God to lead him day by day to those people who needed his message, his actions, his presence. I doubt that he was taken by surprise when Nicodemus showed up, when Pilate was skeptical, when the woman of Samaria happened to be at Jacob's well, when Zacchaeus happened to be in that tree, or when some would-be disciples caught up with him on the road.

I cannot think of many times when I prayed for God to lead me to someone who needed a word of witness from me and that prayer went unanswered. People seem to come into my life (even into my dreams) in answer to that request. I cannot emphasize too strongly that in order to recognize spiritual need in the marketplace, it's absolutely critical that we sharpen our sensitivity in the quiet place.

It is important to note that our subject here is discipleship, not conversion. Christianity is not just a decision, it's a journey into God. It includes a decision, but that decision is the beginning of something. Even as we work to reach people, we also strive to help them grow in discipleship. A couple of years ago, a young man came to my office to talk about baptism and church membership. He had worshiped with us as a child and a teenager. Recently he had been led to meaningful faith through therapy and a twelve-step program. As we discussed the meaning of baptism, I explained to him that it was a church ordinance, not a private ceremony. He would be entering a covenant with a church family that would welcome and nurture him. Frankly and plainly, we talked about how a personal relationship with Christ grows into meaningful discipleship in the fellowship and care of Christ's people. He made his profession of faith the following Sunday, and I baptized him soon thereafter. Since that time, however, I have scarcely seen him in worship or small group Bible study. Perhaps his twelve-step group continues to be a support community for him. For whatever reason, his covenant with our church family is not a priority. Until that covenant becomes a priority for him, with us or with some other faith community, his experience of the fullness of Christ will be severely limited.

In the fall of 1987 the nation followed the saga of eighteen-month-old Jessica McClure of Midland, Texas. She was trapped in an abandoned well for almost sixty hours before she was rescued. What you may not recall is that the rescue was accomplished in two steps. First, they got someone down to where she was, close enough to establish contact with her and to communicate. Then they proceeded to extract her. When you are alone and you feel trapped, hopeless, or uncertain, having someone come to where you are is mighty important. As a church, we can be that someone to one another. If we're going to be disciples, we'll need community.

So where is Jesus to be seen? In the faces and lives and needs of those whom God puts around us and in our path. Pastoral counselor John Reed tells about a man he knew who was experiencing the spiritual emptiness and anxiety of our times. He could no longer believe in the simple Christianity of his youth, yet he was troubled that he could not believe in anything, least of all himself. He started a religious quest, in his words, "to reconsider God." One day he told John, "I got a message from God." Driving home on a snowy, bitterly cold February evening, he had passed a street person wearing no hat or gloves. "I almost stopped my car to give him my gloves," he said, "but then I thought about my thirty-dollar ski gloves and went on home. Still, I couldn't get the image of that man out of my mind." The next morning he called a local department store and made arrangements with the manager to buy three hundred pairs of hats, gloves, and socks, which he delivered to the Salvation Army and the community food kitchen. "The problem is," he said, "it's not enough. I know it's not enough, but maybe God's calling for me is a small one—to be the hat-and-glove man of this town." Someone saw Jesus on the street in the middle of February!

Art Whitmer is a member of our church. Last year he wrote a

letter, put a South Main brochure with it, and delivered copies to each house on his block and on the three blocks around it, contacting ninety-six households altogether. Art's letter introduces him as a neighbor. He talks about kids and families, about a pressure-cooker lifestyle, about the need for relationships and pizzazz in daily life, and for help in dealing with today's issues. He speaks of how life can be enriched and blessed by faith and by his church. "Here's my phone number," he writes. "If you've got questions about South Main Baptist Church, about transportation, about how to join a dynamic faith community, call me." He is delivering these letters door-to-door. Starting in his immediate neighborhood, he plans to take them to all six thousand households in his community. Someone saw Jesus in a Houston neighborhood in the springtime of 1995!

Kenneth and Nelda Lawrence were among several South Main couples who have carried on a very substantial ministry to the international students of our city over the years. One day shortly after World War II, Kenneth was at Rice University looking for a young Japanese student. As he searched for that young man, he happened upon some other students who were studying. A stack of books that included a Bible was on the table in front of them. Kenneth introduced himself and asked what they were doing. "We're discussing the authors of these books." Pointing to the Bible, Kenneth asked, "Do you know the author of this book?" One student said, "Nobody can know the author of that book."

"Yes, you can!" said Kenneth. "Let me tell you about that author." Kenneth quickly told them the story of God's love, culminating with the Jesus story. He wound up his visit by saying, "I want to invite all of you to come to my church next Sunday. It's South Main Baptist Church, just down the street." When university and international invitees like this showed up at our church on Sundays, Kenneth and Nelda would often meet them, sit with them, and take them to Sunday lunch. Some of those young adults came to Christian faith and church membership through the diligence of the Lawrences' campus contacts. Someone saw Jesus in a college dorm room in the 1940s!

The faith sharers in the New Testament are not professional clergy. They are farmers and tax collectors, lawyers and fishermen, merchants and doctors, teachers and tent makers. They are people who see everyday life as the arena for witness and ministry. They had a good model for that, and so do we—Jesus, a faith sharer *par excellence*!

Epilogue

We Christians are called to address the spiritual hunger and thirst of the 1990s and beyond. In the midst of a spiritually starving culture we are bearers of bread. Into the darkness of violence and evil we are bearers of light. We are prodigal children who have found our way back home and can tell others how to find it.

But this enormous and important task of personal witness is not ours alone. The risen Christ is our partner in sharing grace, making disciples, and living a faith that is believable to those around us. Jesus' own faith sharing provides effective teaching and encouragement for this task. It is a source that we can draw on again and again.

There is a transparency in Jesus' encounters with people that invites them to let themselves be loved and changed by God. I also see a strong intentionality in these encounters. Jesus would find a way to listen, to understand the particular human situation, and to articulate his word about a loving, life-changing God.

I continue to be inspired by Jesus' model and by the model of those in our own time who follow his example. The story of a Colombian woman named Dona Maria bears telling. Her friend, missionary Marion Corley, visited us in Houston in the fall of 1994. Marion wrote a book detailing twenty years of missionary service in Colombia. The faithful Dona Maria plays a major role in Marion's story.

Dona Maria was old, and her eyesight was growing dim. She wanted to share her faith in Christ with others, but how could an illiterate, often forgetful person do that? As she left church one Sunday, she took a gospel tract and started home. She prayed that

God would lead her to someone who needed her witness. Soon she "happened" to see a man, a complete stranger, who was building his house. Approaching him she said, "Mister, can you read?" He answered, "Why, sure!" She said, "I got this paper at church, but I can't read. Would you read it to me?" The man laid aside his hammer and started to read the tract aloud to Dona Maria. It said that all of us are sinners. "That's bad news, isn't it?" she said. The man continued to read about how God loves us despite the fact that we are sinners. "I'm glad to hear that," the old woman said. The man went on to read about how Jesus came to earth to live and die for our sins. "That's good news, isn't it?" she exclaimed. Then the tract explained that confessing our sins and asking for God's forgiveness leads to salvation and eternal life. At that point Dona Maria said, "That's the best news I've ever heard!" The man folded the tract and started to hand it back to the old woman. "Why don't you keep it," she said, "since I can't read." And she walked away toward her home.[1]

Who knows if that man ever became a believer or not? Like most stories of faith sharing, it remains unfinished. I wish we knew the rest of it. The point is that Dona Maria found a way to share her faith. Illiterate, old, forgetful, and untutored in the techniques of personal evangelism, she found a way to share the story. Anyone reading Dona Maria's story is far better equipped educationally than she.

But I wonder how many are as intentional as she. It is my hope that revisiting Jesus' faith-sharing encounters has challenged us afresh and has set us free to follow his lead!

Note

1. Marion Corley, *Dona Maria and Friends* (Birmingham, Ala.: New Hope, 1991), p. 28.